# MAKER COMICS

# SURVIVE IN THE OUTDOORS!

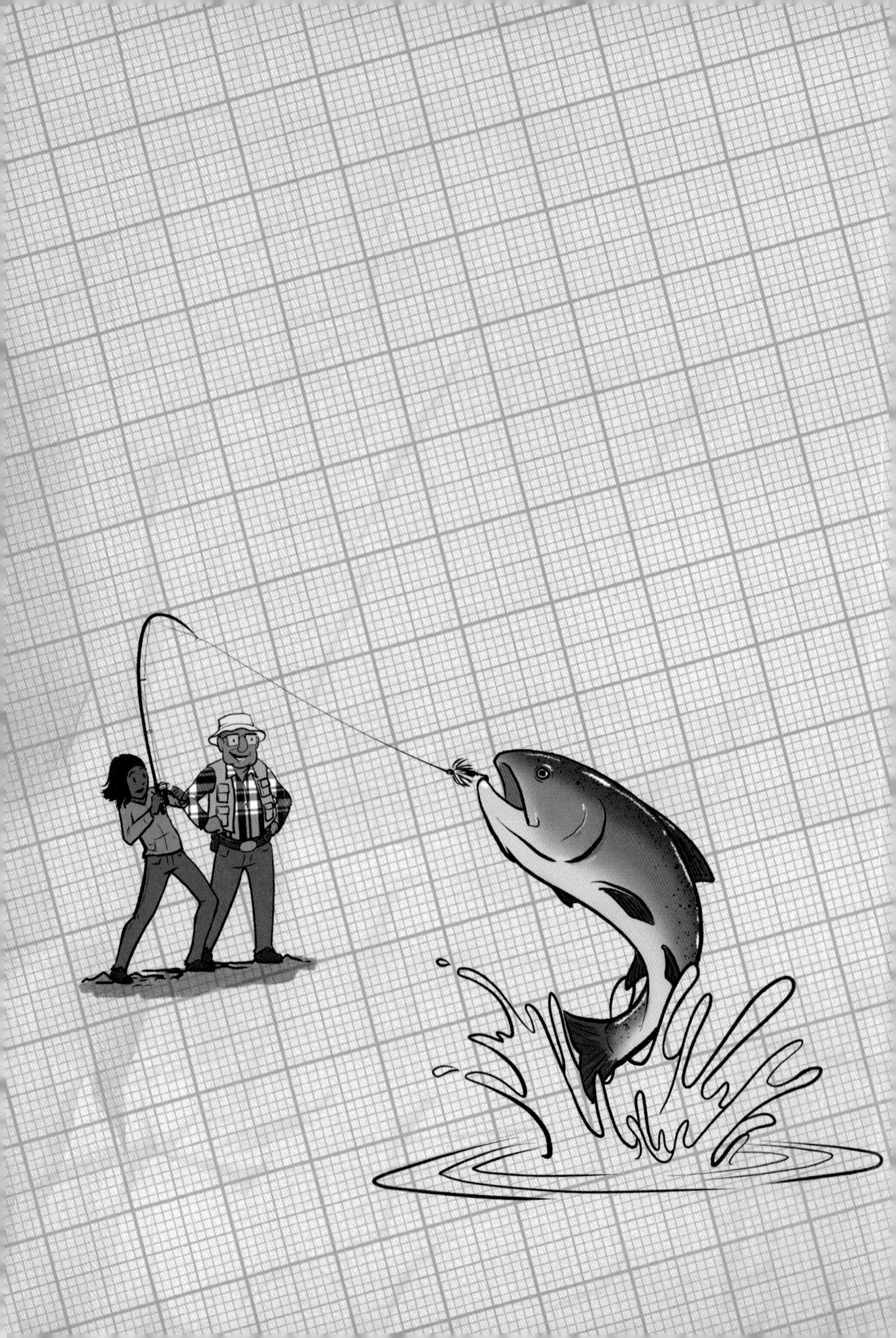

# SURVIVE IN THE OUTDOORS!

## Mike Lawrence

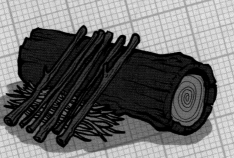

:01

First Second
New York

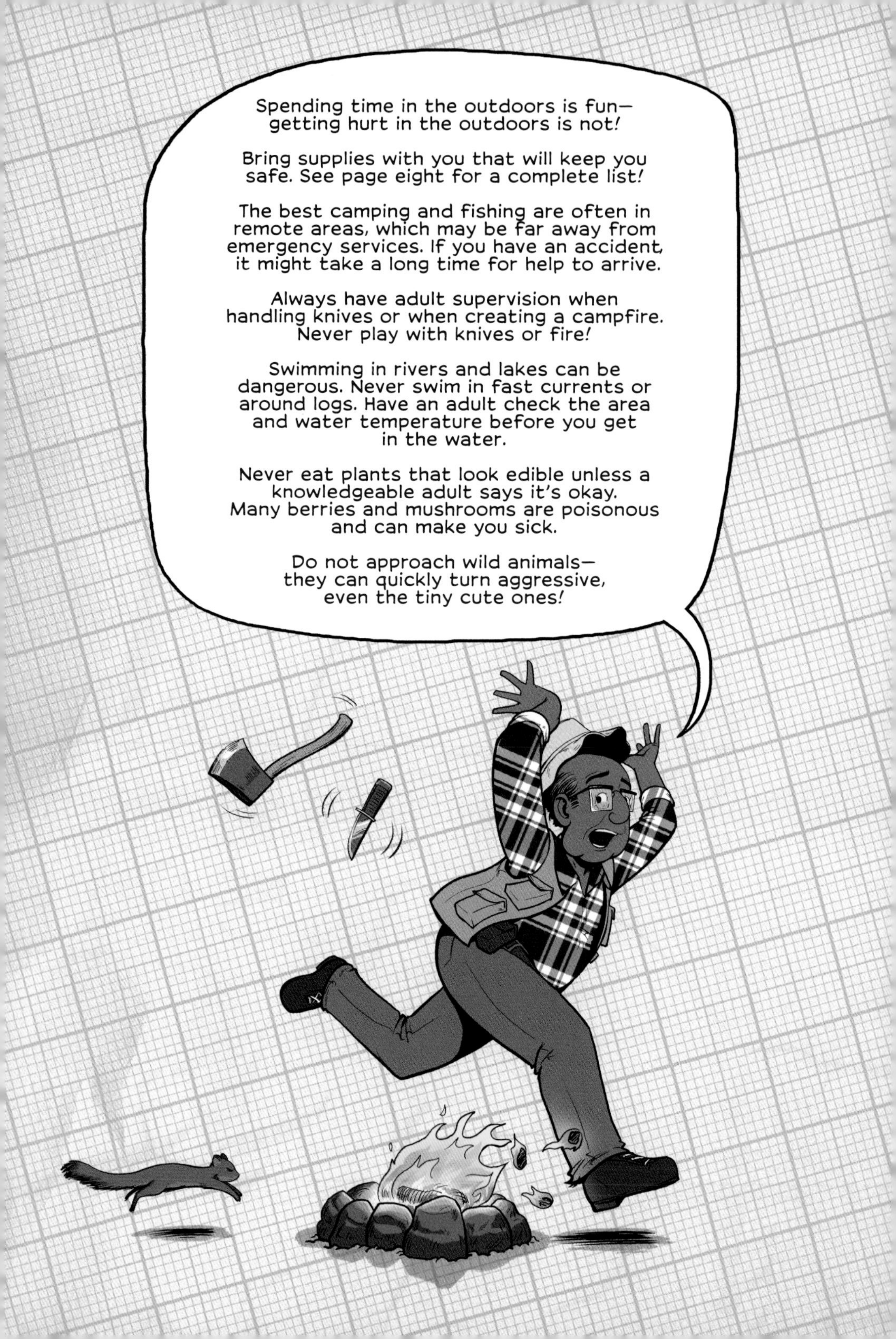
Spending time in the outdoors is fun—getting hurt in the outdoors is not!
Bring supplies with you that will keep you safe. See page eight for a complete list!
The best camping and fishing are often in remote areas, which may be far away from emergency services. If you have an accident, it might take a long time for help to arrive.
Always have adult supervision when handling knives or when creating a campfire. Never play with knives or fire!
Swimming in rivers and lakes can be dangerous. Never swim in fast currents or around logs. Have an adult check the area and water temperature before you get in the water.
Never eat plants that look edible unless a knowledgeable adult says it's okay. Many berries and mushrooms are poisonous and can make you sick.
Do not approach wild animals—they can quickly turn aggressive, even the tiny cute ones!

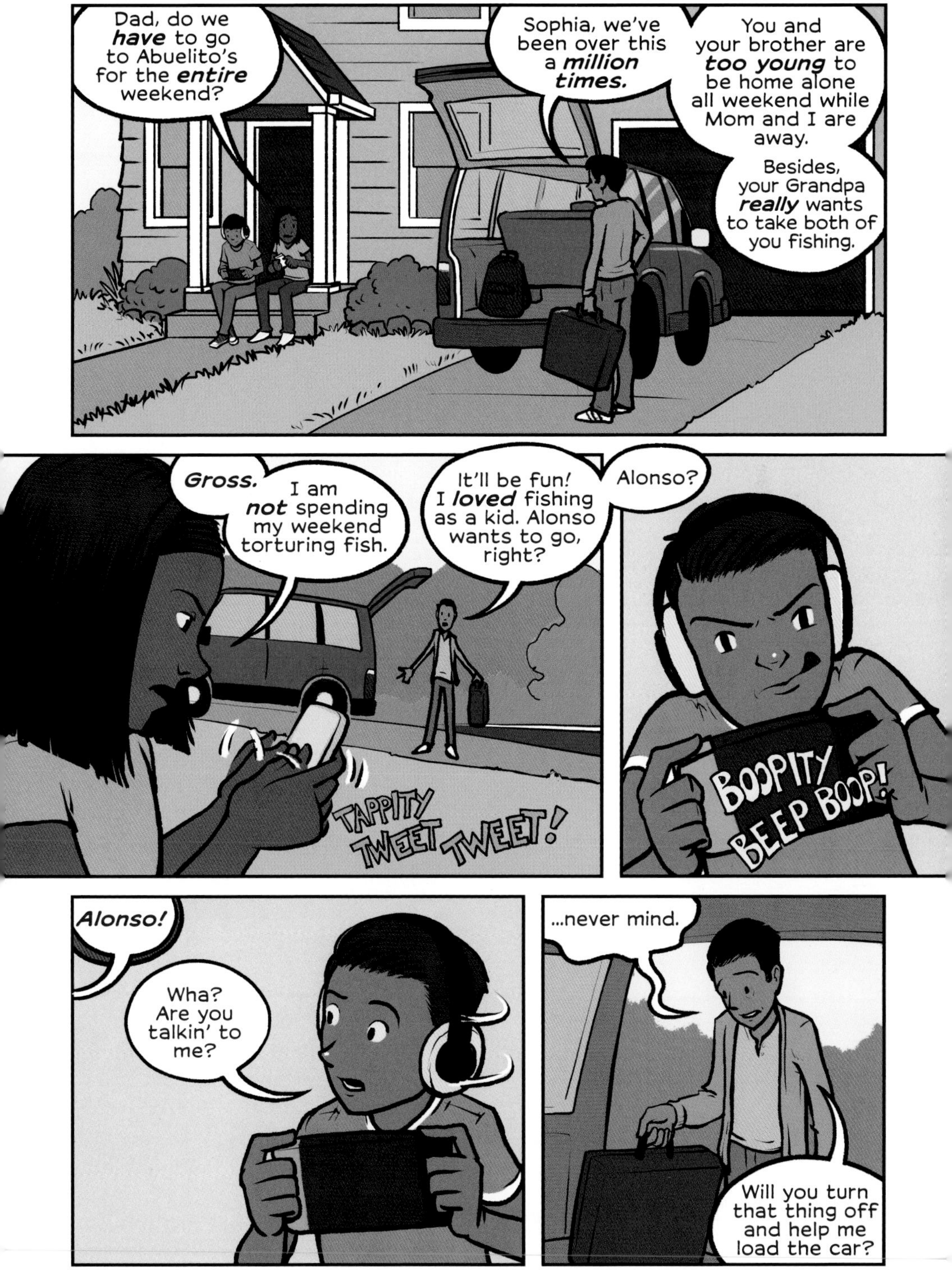

Dad, do we *have* to go to Abuelito's for the *entire* weekend?
Sophia, we've been over this a *million times.*
You and your brother are *too young* to be home alone all weekend while Mom and I are away.
Besides, your Grandpa *really* wants to take both of you fishing.
*Gross.*
I am *not* spending my weekend torturing fish.
TAPPITY TWEET TWEET!
It'll be fun! I *loved* fishing as a kid. Alonso wants to go, right?
Alonso?
BOOPITY BEEP BOOP!
*Alonso!*
Wha? Are you talkin' to me?
...never mind.
Will you turn that thing off and help me load the car?

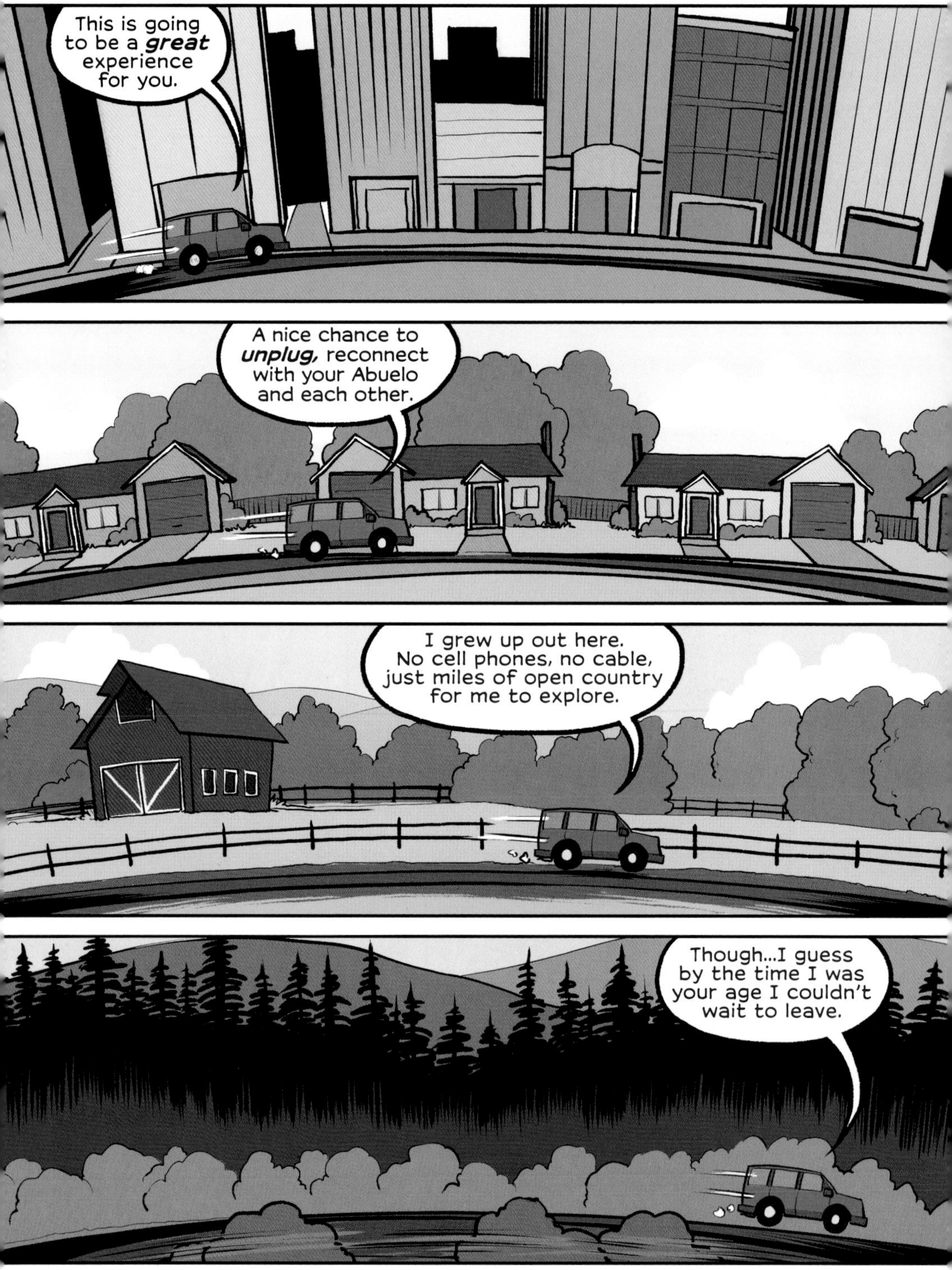
This is going to be a ***great*** experience for you.
A nice chance to ***unplug,*** reconnect with your Abuelo and each other.
I grew up out here. No cell phones, no cable, just miles of open country for me to explore.
Though...I guess by the time I was your age I couldn't wait to leave.

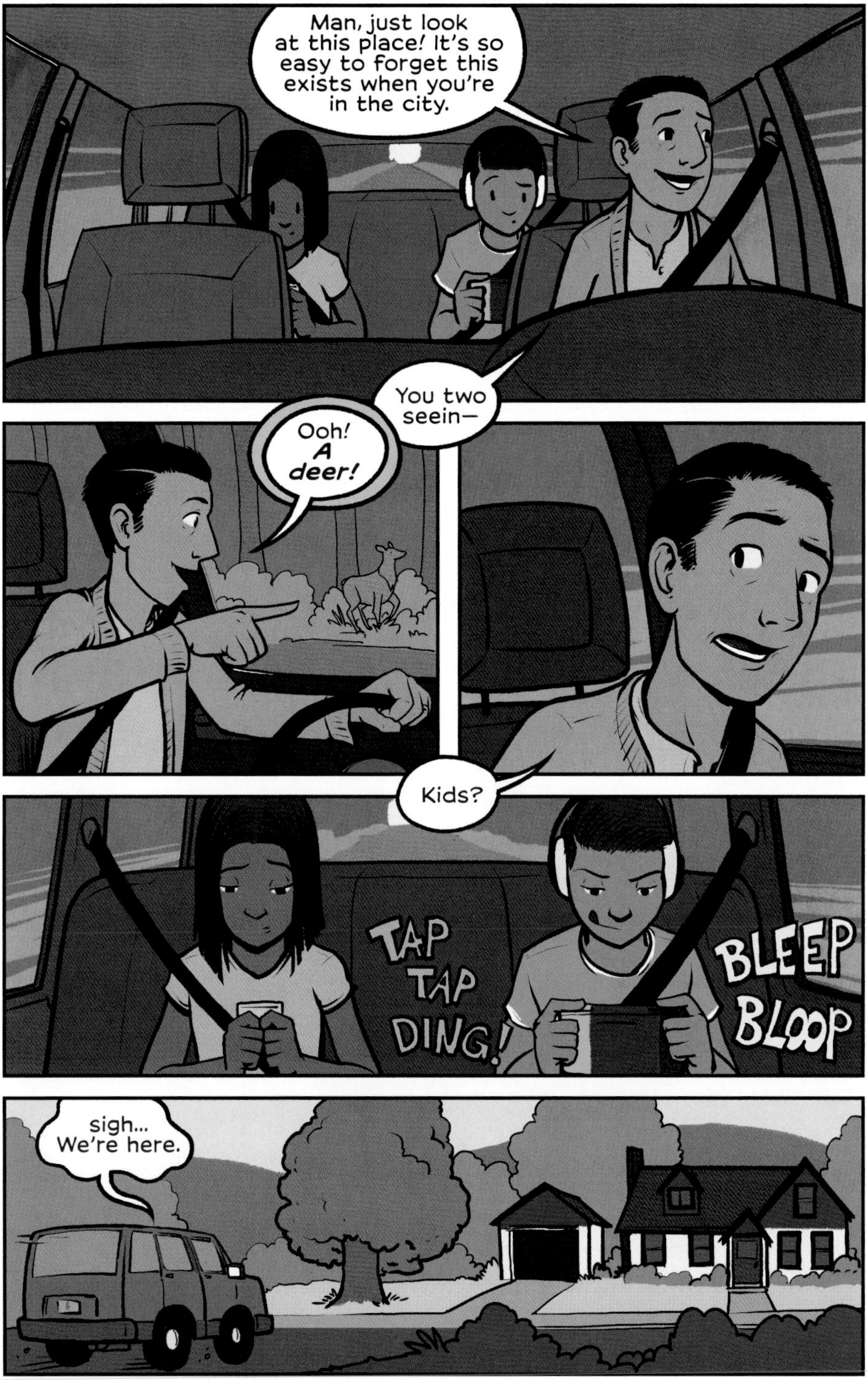
Man, just look at this place! It's so easy to forget this exists when you're in the city.
You two seein—
Ooh! A deer!
Kids?
TAP TAP DING!
BLEEP BLOOP
sigh... We're here.

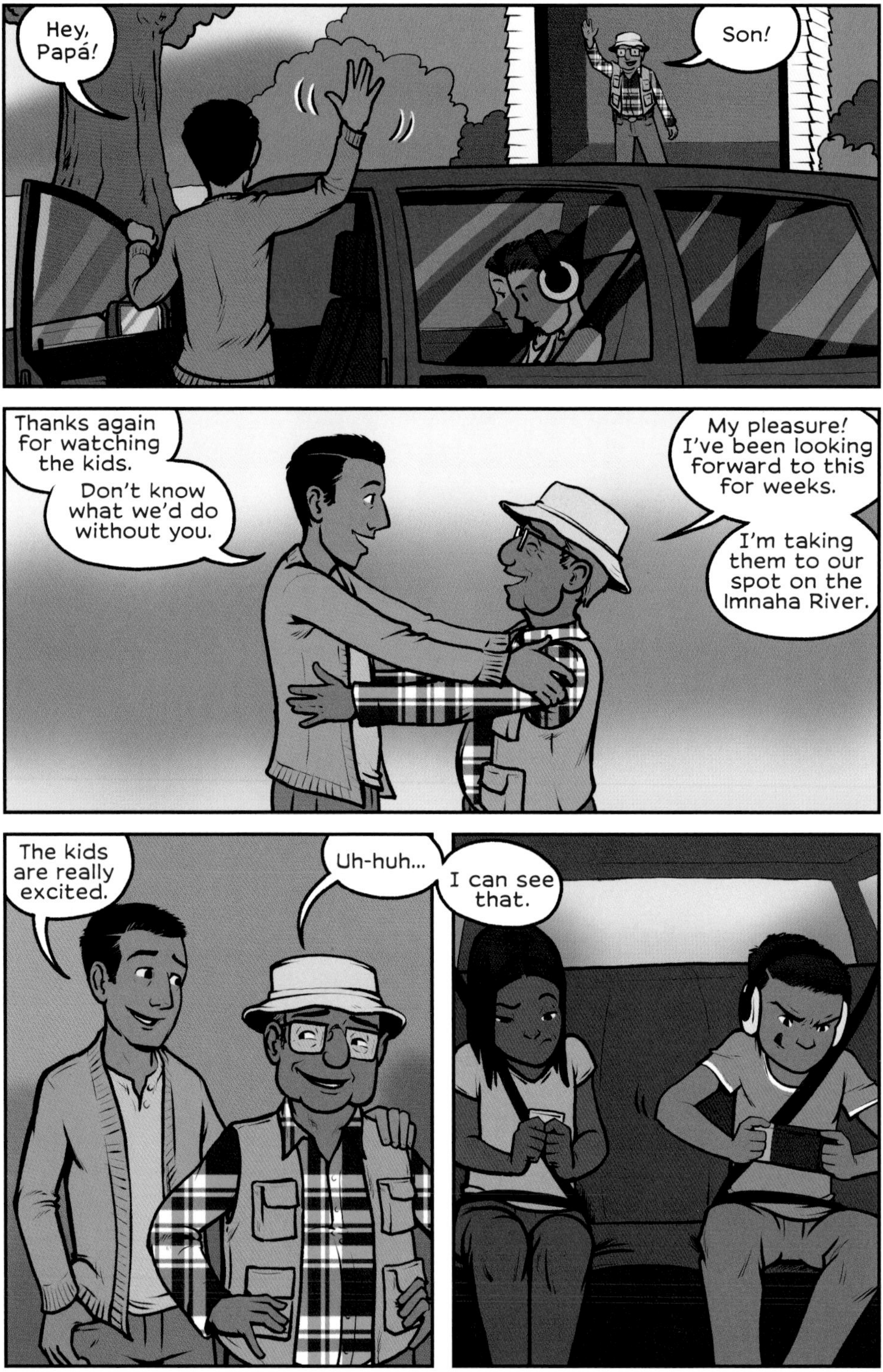
Hey, Papá!
Son!
Thanks again for watching the kids.
Don't know what we'd do without you.
My pleasure! I've been looking forward to this for weeks.
I'm taking them to our spot on the Imnaha River.
The kids are really excited.
Uh-huh...
I can see that.

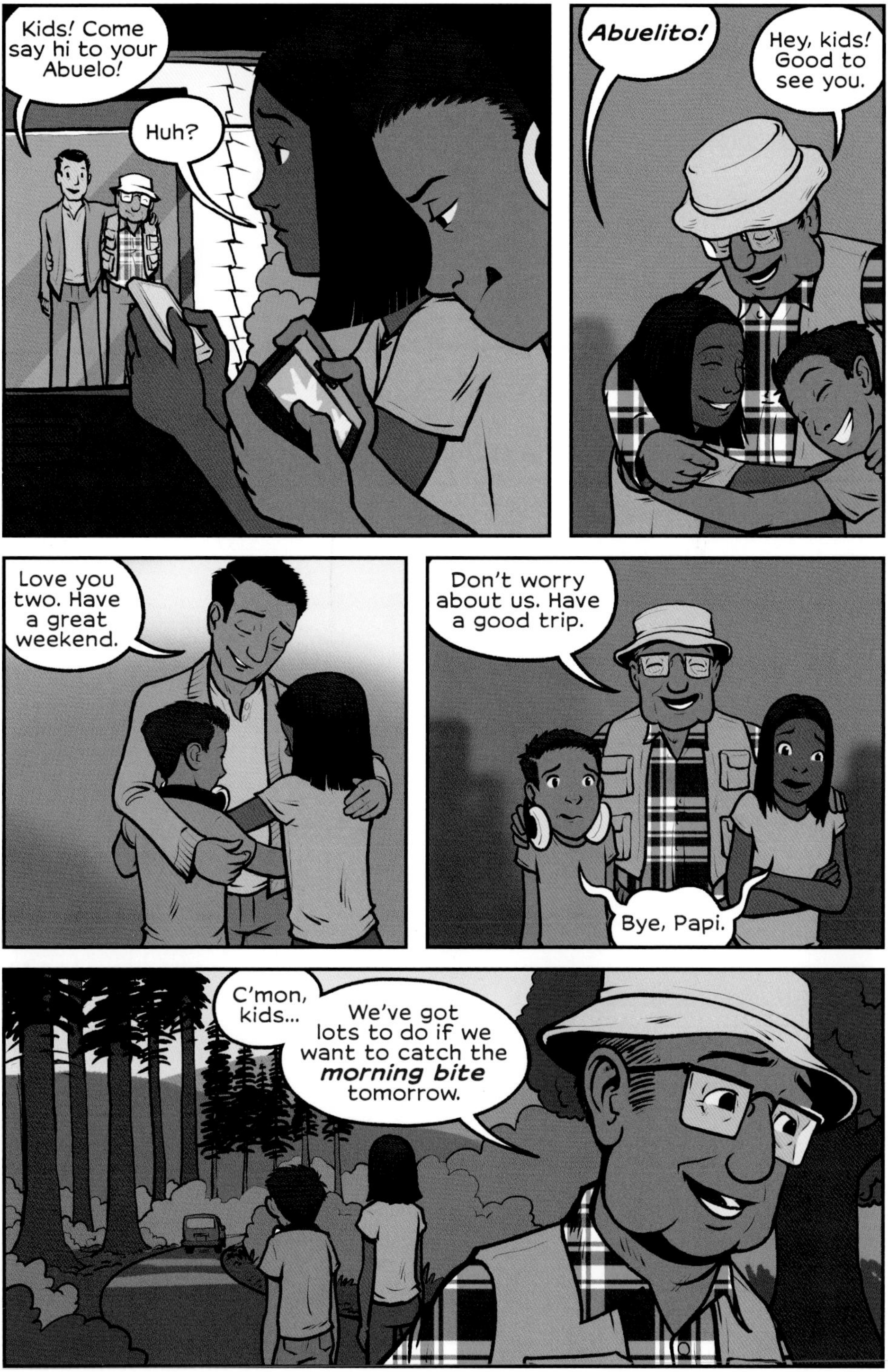
Kids! Come say hi to your Abuelo!
Huh?
Abuelito!
Hey, kids! Good to see you.
Love you two. Have a great weekend.
Don't worry about us. Have a good trip.
Bye, Papi.
C'mon, kids...
We've got lots to do if we want to catch the *morning bite* tomorrow.

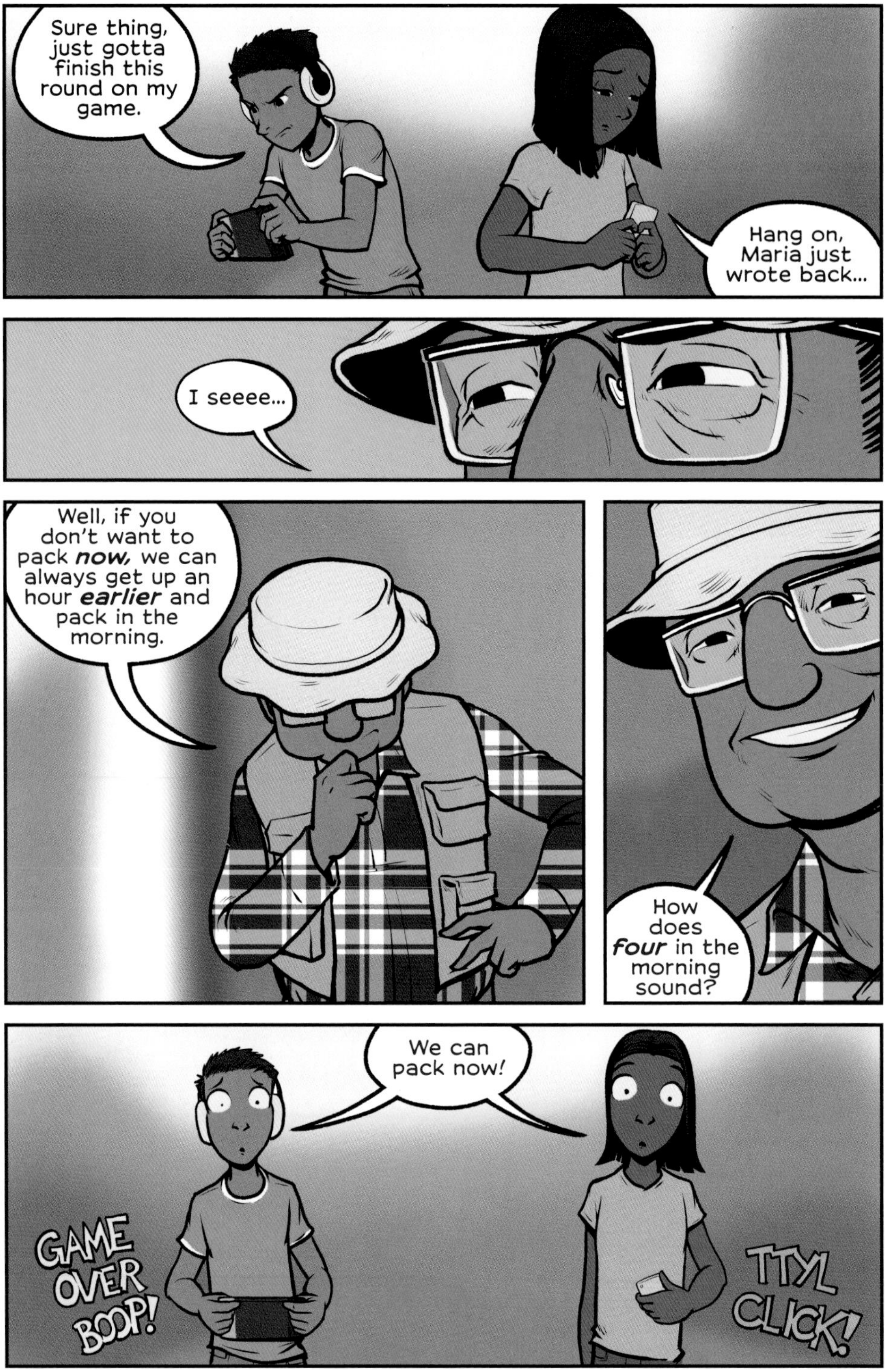
Sure thing, just gotta finish this round on my game.
Hang on, Maria just wrote back...
I seeee...
Well, if you don't want to pack *now,* we can always get up an hour *earlier* and pack in the morning.
How does *four* in the morning sound?
We can pack now!
GAME OVER BOOP!
TTYL CLICK!

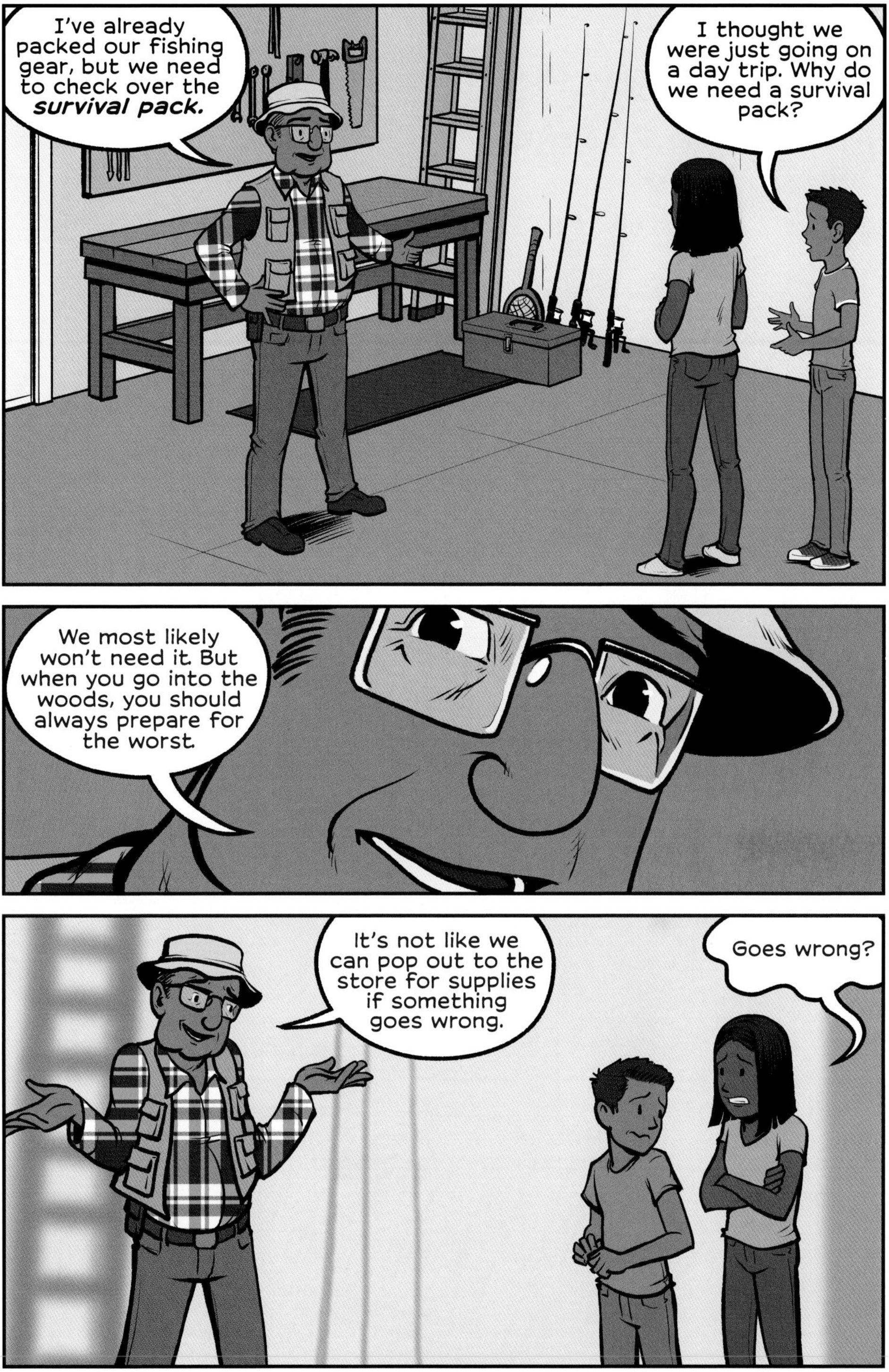
I've already packed our fishing gear, but we need to check over the *survival pack.*
I thought we were just going on a day trip. Why do we need a survival pack?
We most likely won't need it. But when you go into the woods, you should always prepare for the worst.
It's not like we can pop out to the store for supplies if something goes wrong.
Goes wrong?

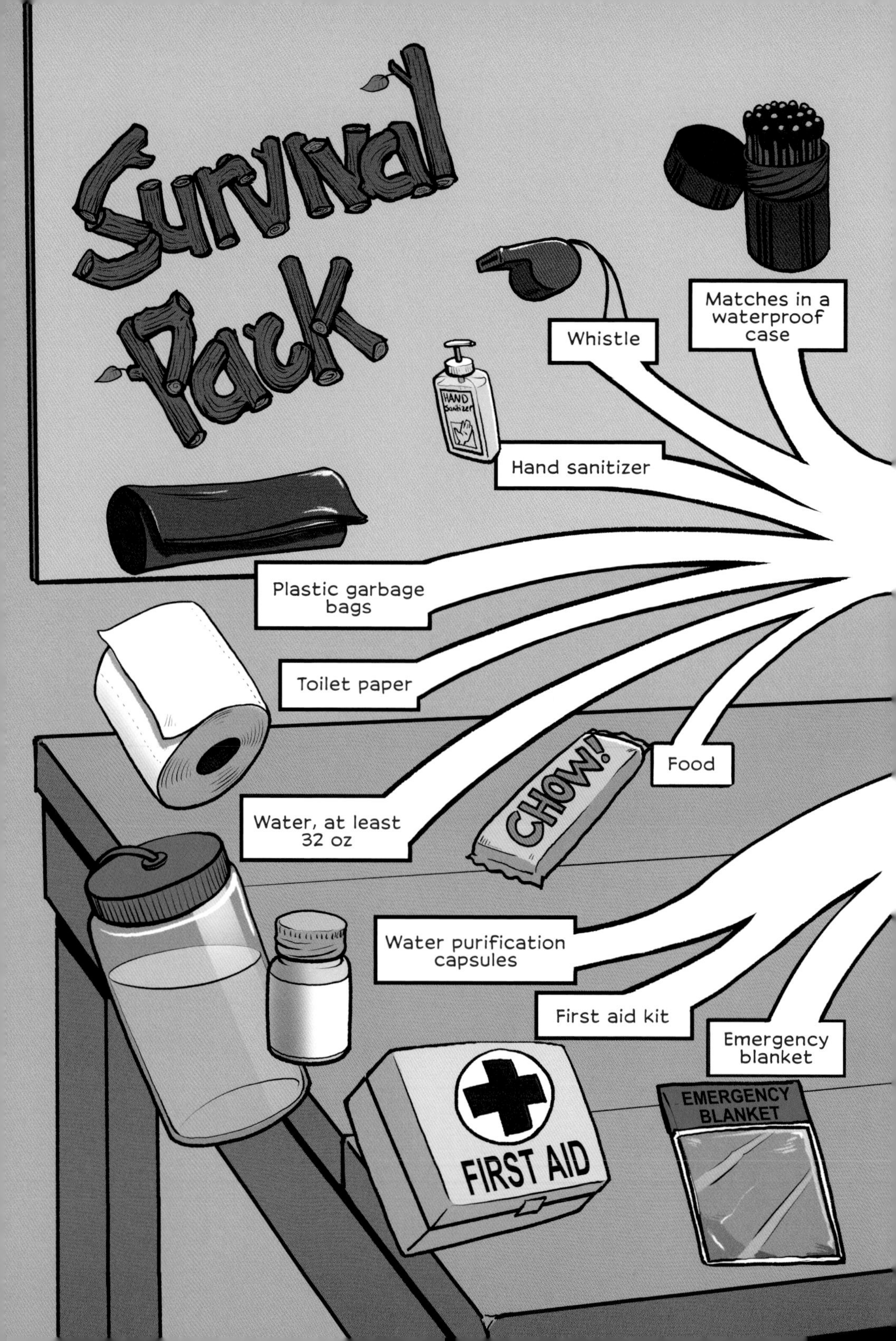
Survival Pack
Matches in a waterproof case
Whistle
HAND Sanitizer
Hand sanitizer
Plastic garbage bags
Toilet paper
Food
CHOW!
Water, at least 32 oz
Water purification capsules
First aid kit
Emergency blanket
FIRST AID
EMERGENCY BLANKET

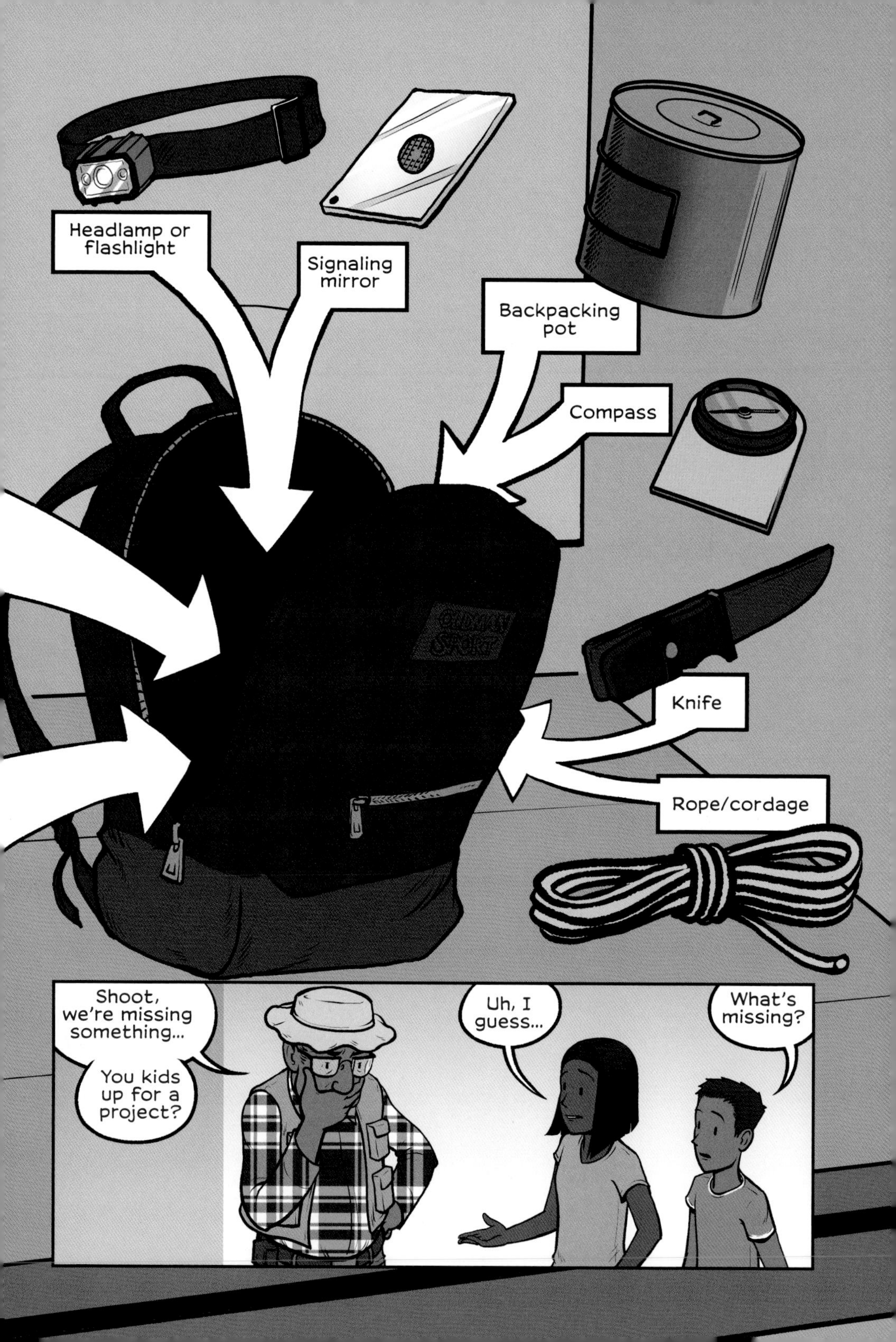
Headlamp or flashlight
Signaling mirror
Backpacking pot
Compass
Knife
Rope/cordage
Shoot, we're missing something...
You kids up for a project?
Uh, I guess...
What's missing?

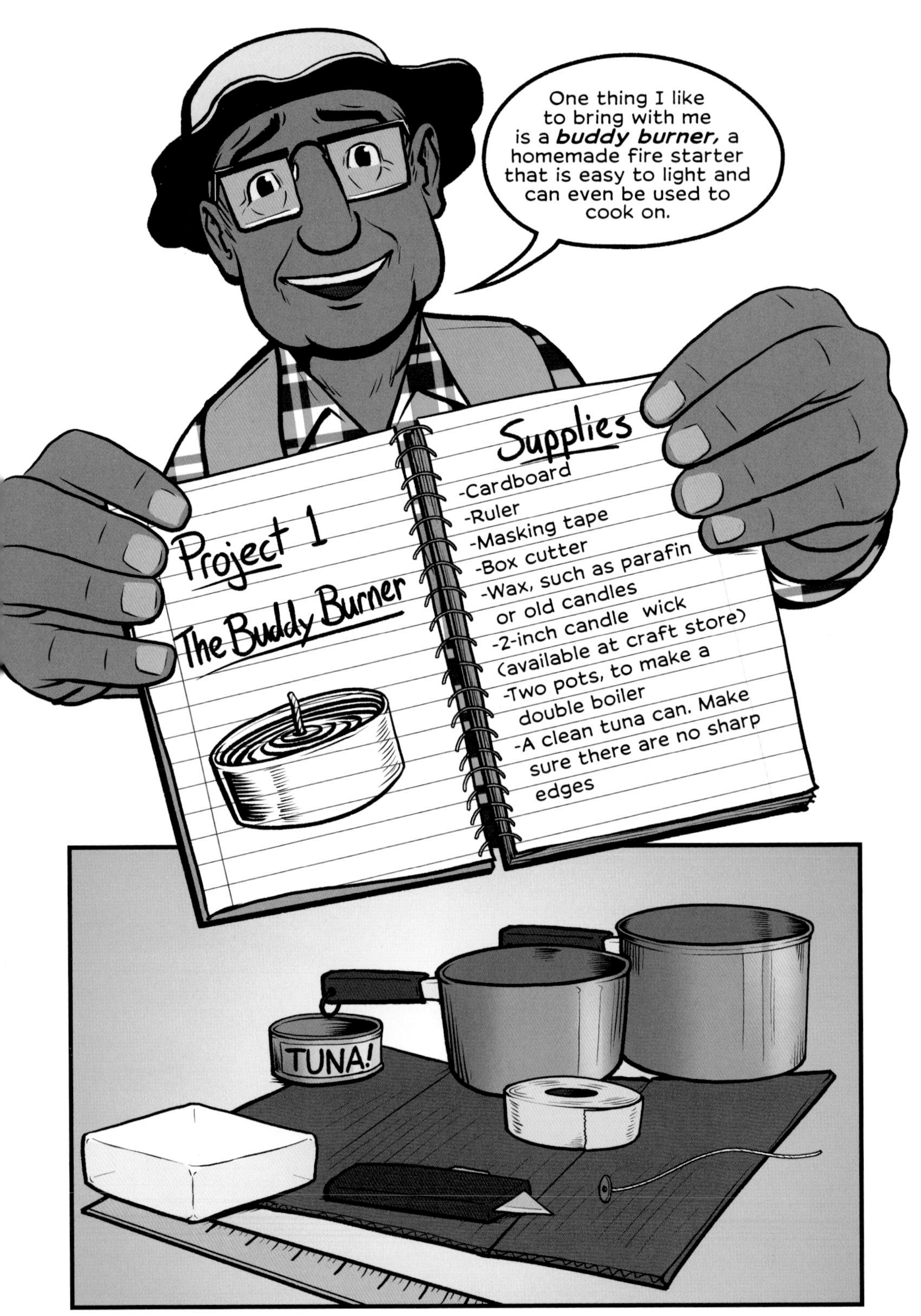
One thing I like to bring with me is a ***buddy burner,*** a homemade fire starter that is easy to light and can even be used to cook on.
Project 1
The Buddy Burner
Supplies
-Cardboard
-Ruler
-Masking tape
-Box cutter
-Wax, such as parafin or old candles
-2-inch candle wick (available at craft store)
-Two pots, to make a double boiler
-A clean tuna can. Make sure there are no sharp edges
TUNA!

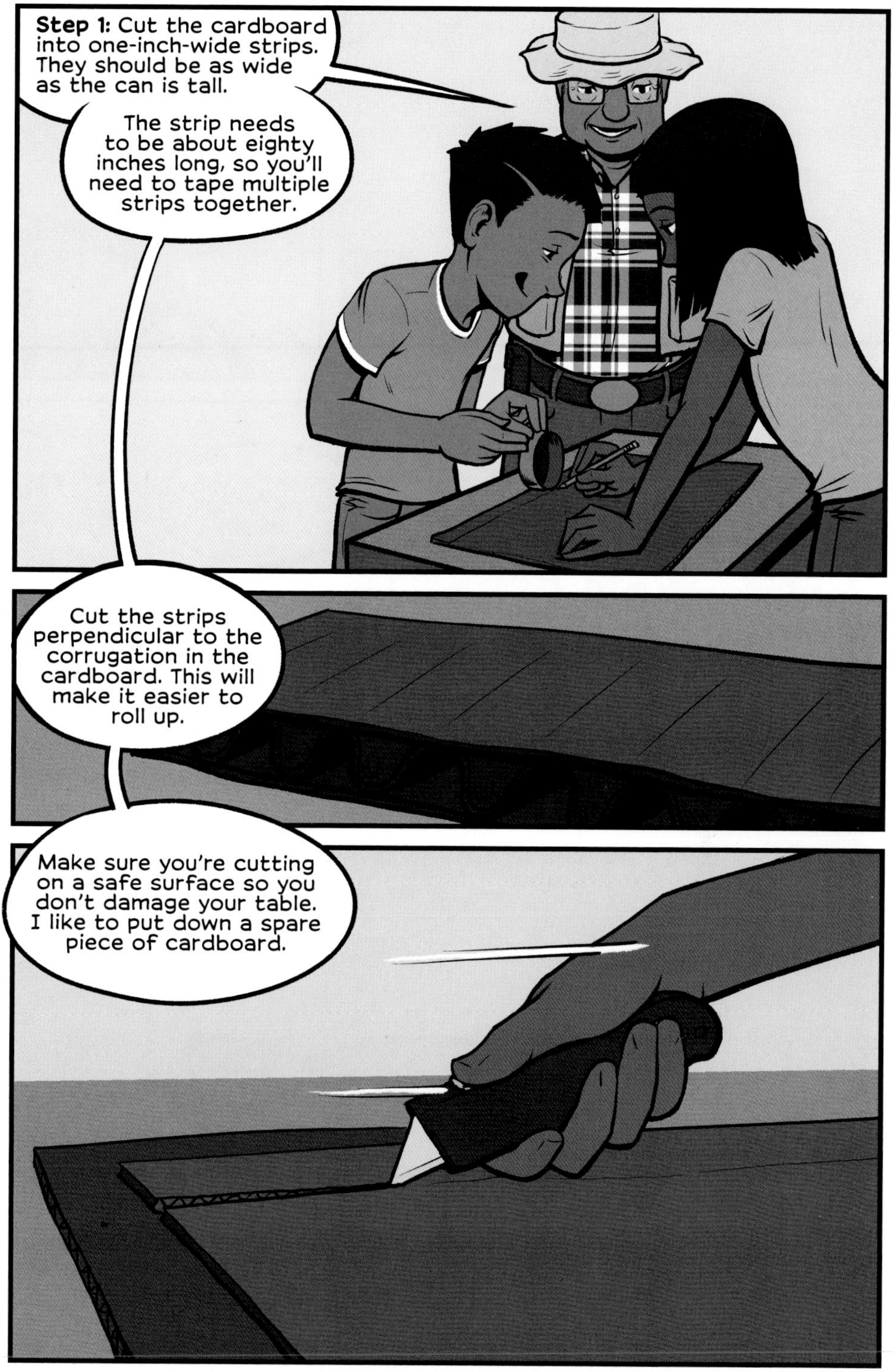
**Step 1:** Cut the cardboard into one-inch-wide strips. They should be as wide as the can is tall.
The strip needs to be about eighty inches long, so you'll need to tape multiple strips together.
Cut the strips perpendicular to the corrugation in the cardboard. This will make it easier to roll up.
Make sure you're cutting on a safe surface so you don't damage your table. I like to put down a spare piece of cardboard.

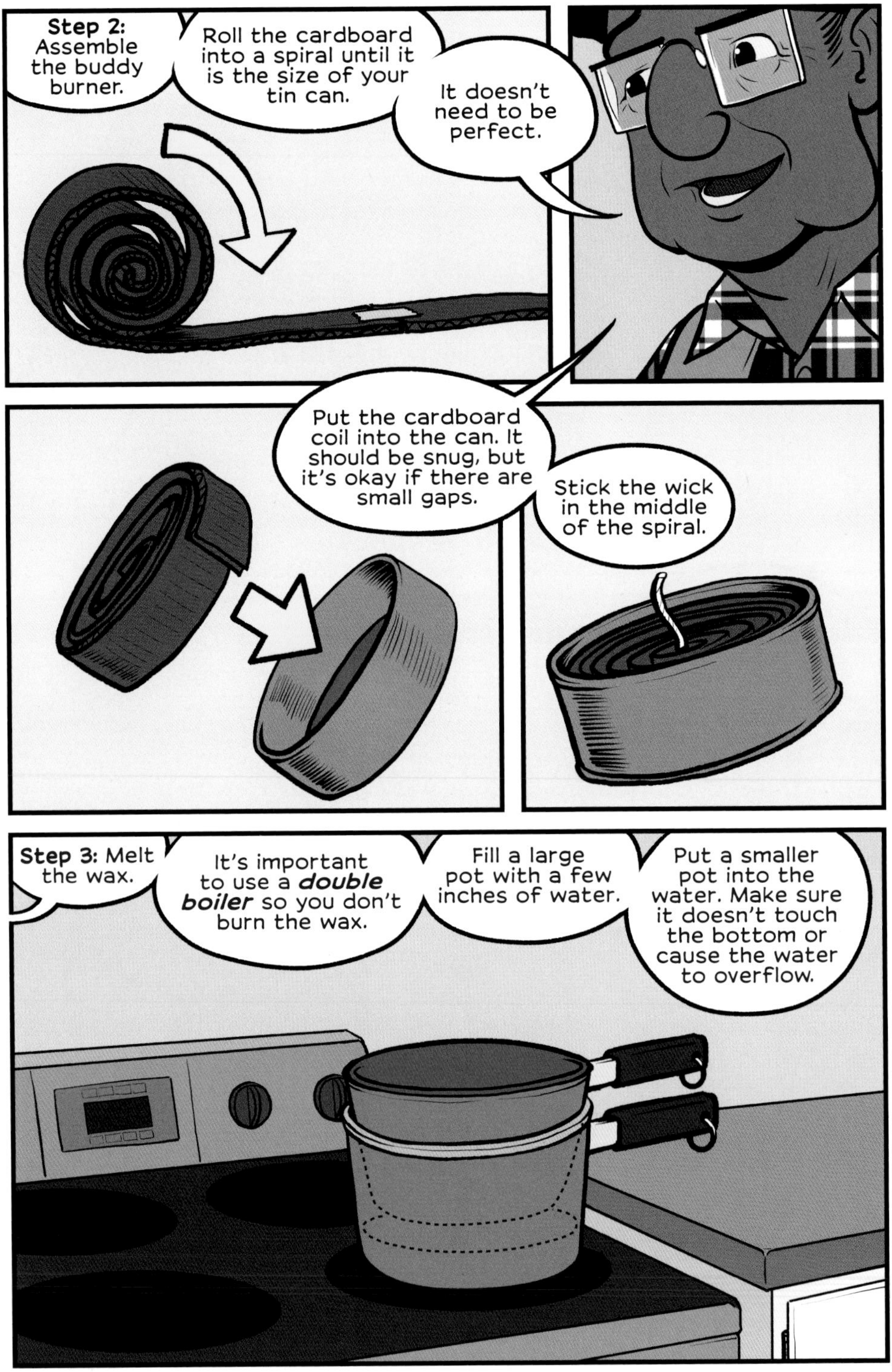
Step 2: Assemble the buddy burner.
Roll the cardboard into a spiral until it is the size of your tin can.
It doesn't need to be perfect.
Put the cardboard coil into the can. It should be snug, but it's okay if there are small gaps.
Stick the wick in the middle of the spiral.
Step 3: Melt the wax.
It's important to use a ***double boiler*** so you don't burn the wax.
Fill a large pot with a few inches of water.
Put a smaller pot into the water. Make sure it doesn't touch the bottom or cause the water to overflow.

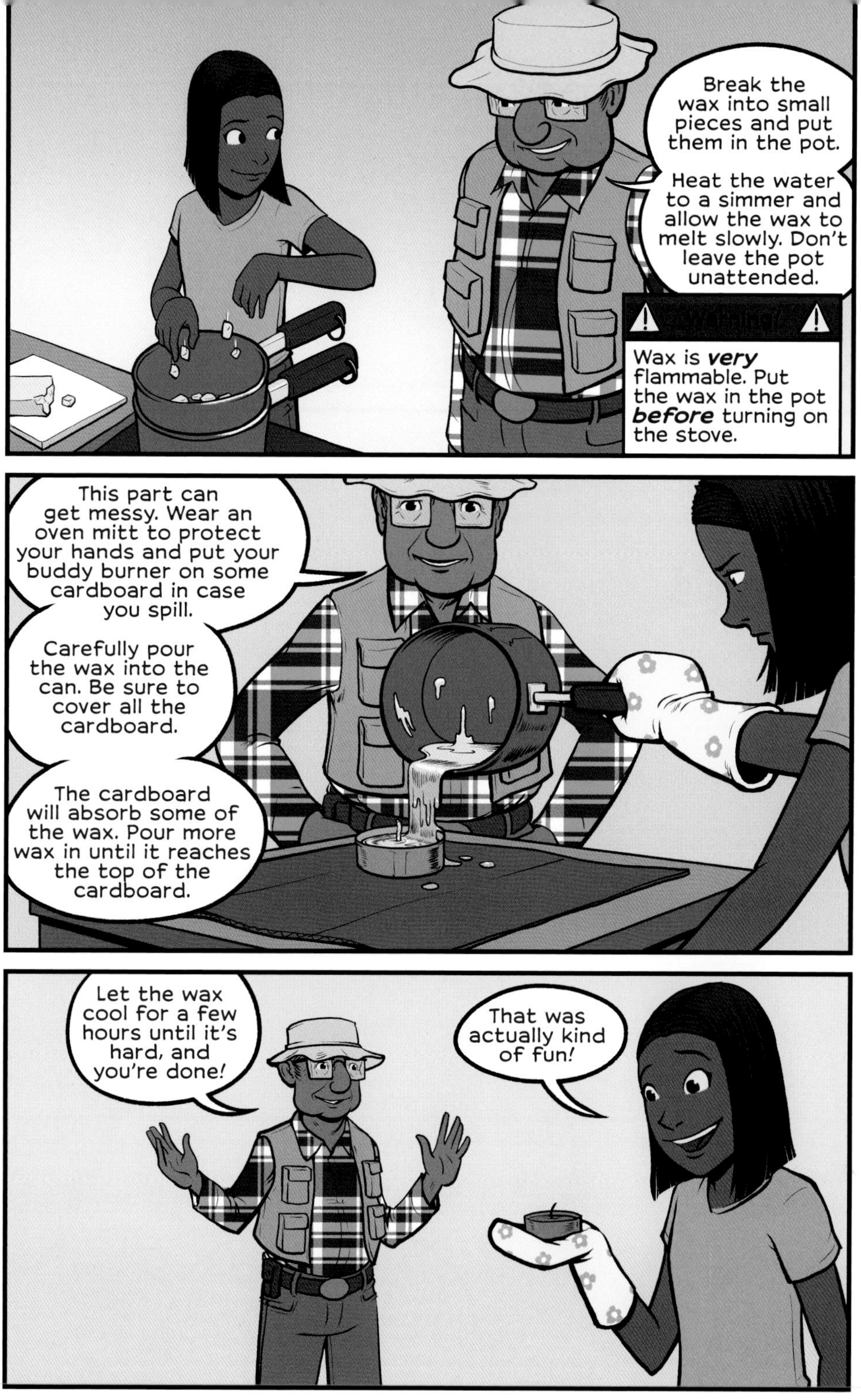
Break the wax into small pieces and put them in the pot.
Heat the water to a simmer and allow the wax to melt slowly. Don't leave the pot unattended.
Wax is ***very*** flammable. Put the wax in the pot ***before*** turning on the stove.
This part can get messy. Wear an oven mitt to protect your hands and put your buddy burner on some cardboard in case you spill.
Carefully pour the wax into the can. Be sure to cover all the cardboard.
The cardboard will absorb some of the wax. Pour more wax in until it reaches the top of the cardboard.
Let the wax cool for a few hours until it's hard, and you're done!
That was actually kind of fun!

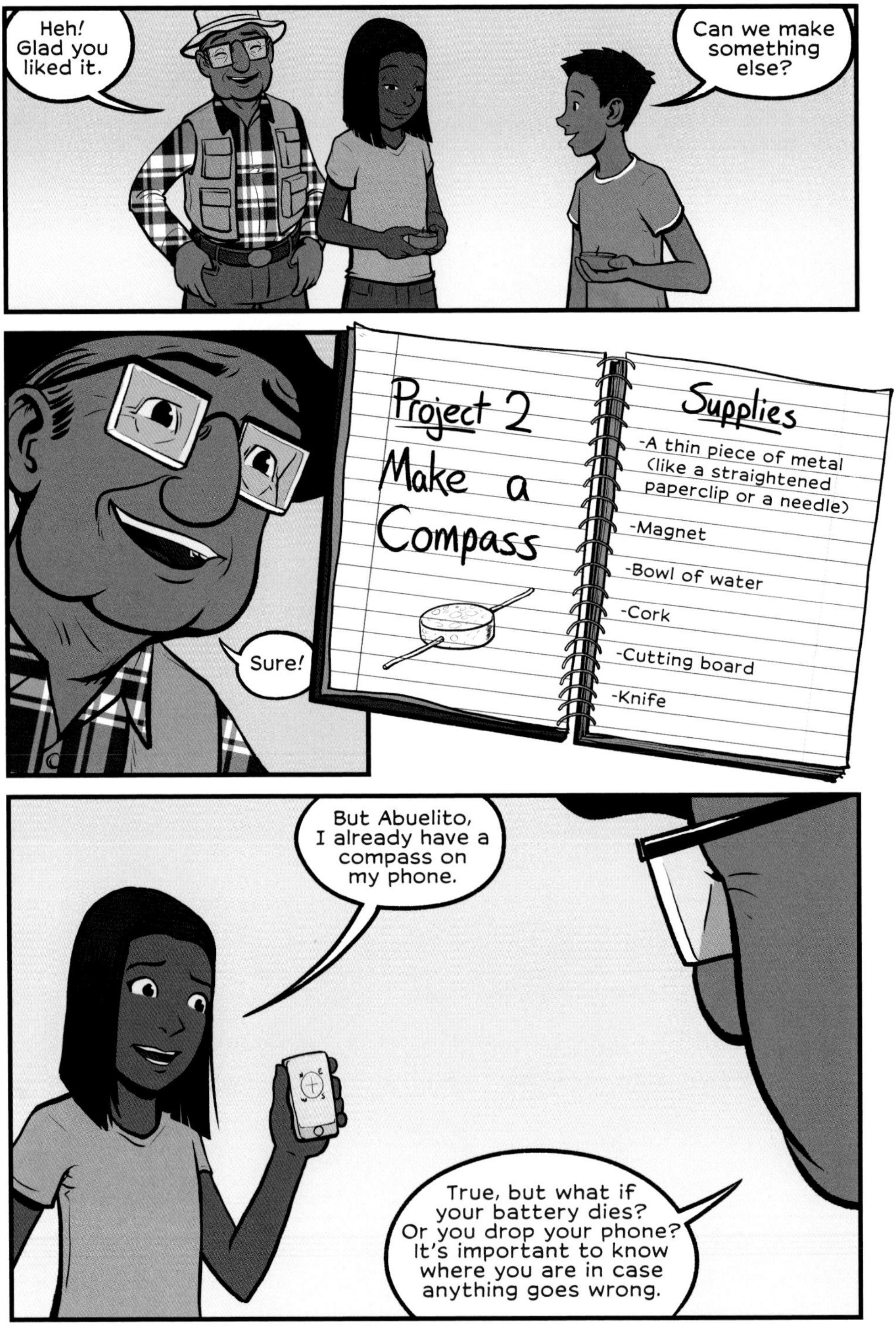

Heh! Glad you liked it.
Can we make something else?
Sure!
Project 2
Make a Compass
Supplies
-A thin piece of metal (like a straightened paperclip or a needle)
-Magnet
-Bowl of water
-Cork
-Cutting board
-Knife
But Abuelito, I already have a compass on my phone.
True, but what if your battery dies? Or you drop your phone? It's important to know where you are in case anything goes wrong.

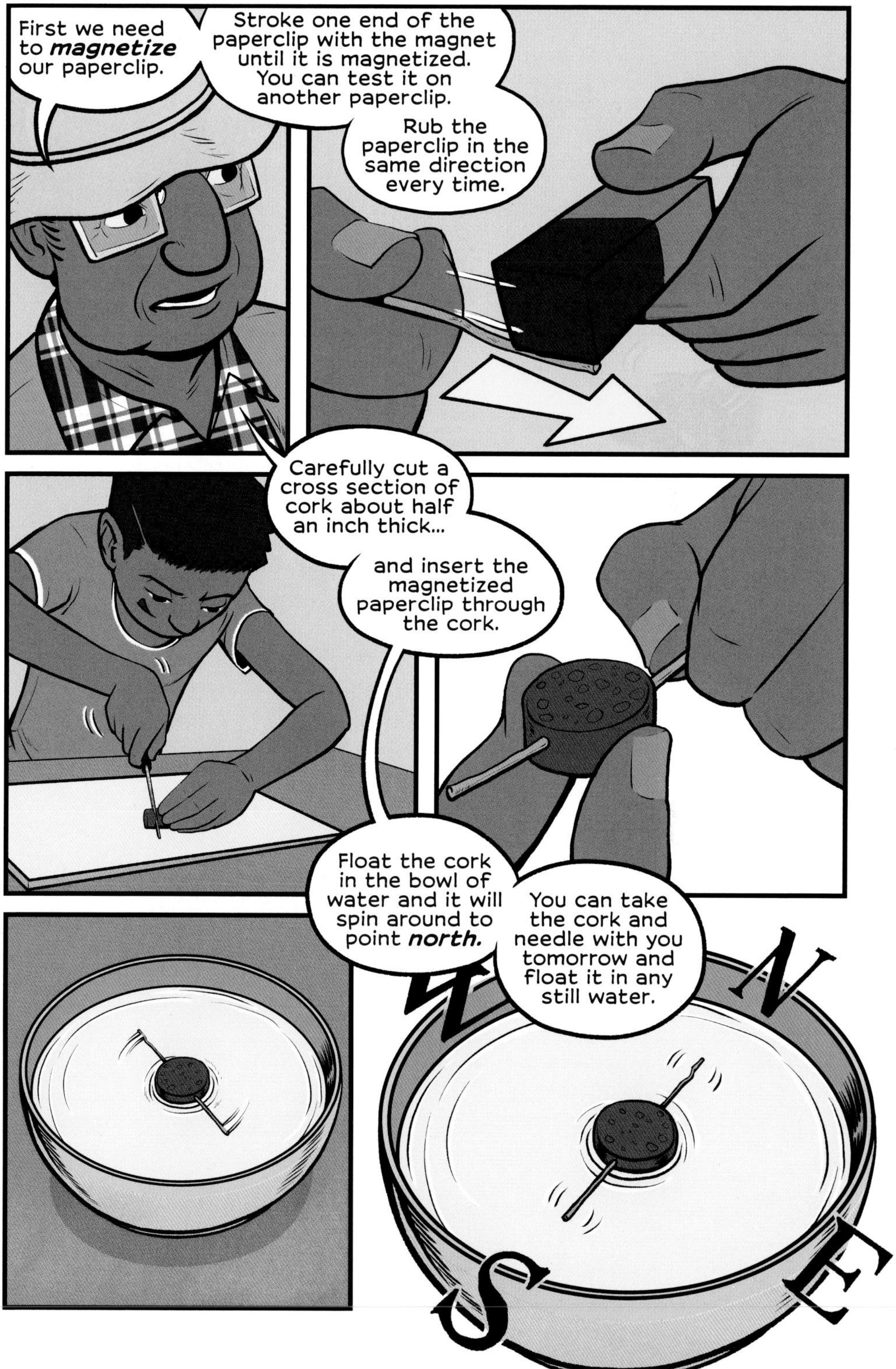
First we need to ***magnetize*** our paperclip.
Stroke one end of the paperclip with the magnet until it is magnetized. You can test it on another paperclip.
Rub the paperclip in the same direction every time.
Carefully cut a cross section of cork about half an inch thick...
and insert the magnetized paperclip through the cork.
Float the cork in the bowl of water and it will spin around to point ***north.***
You can take the cork and needle with you tomorrow and float it in any still water.
N
W
S
E

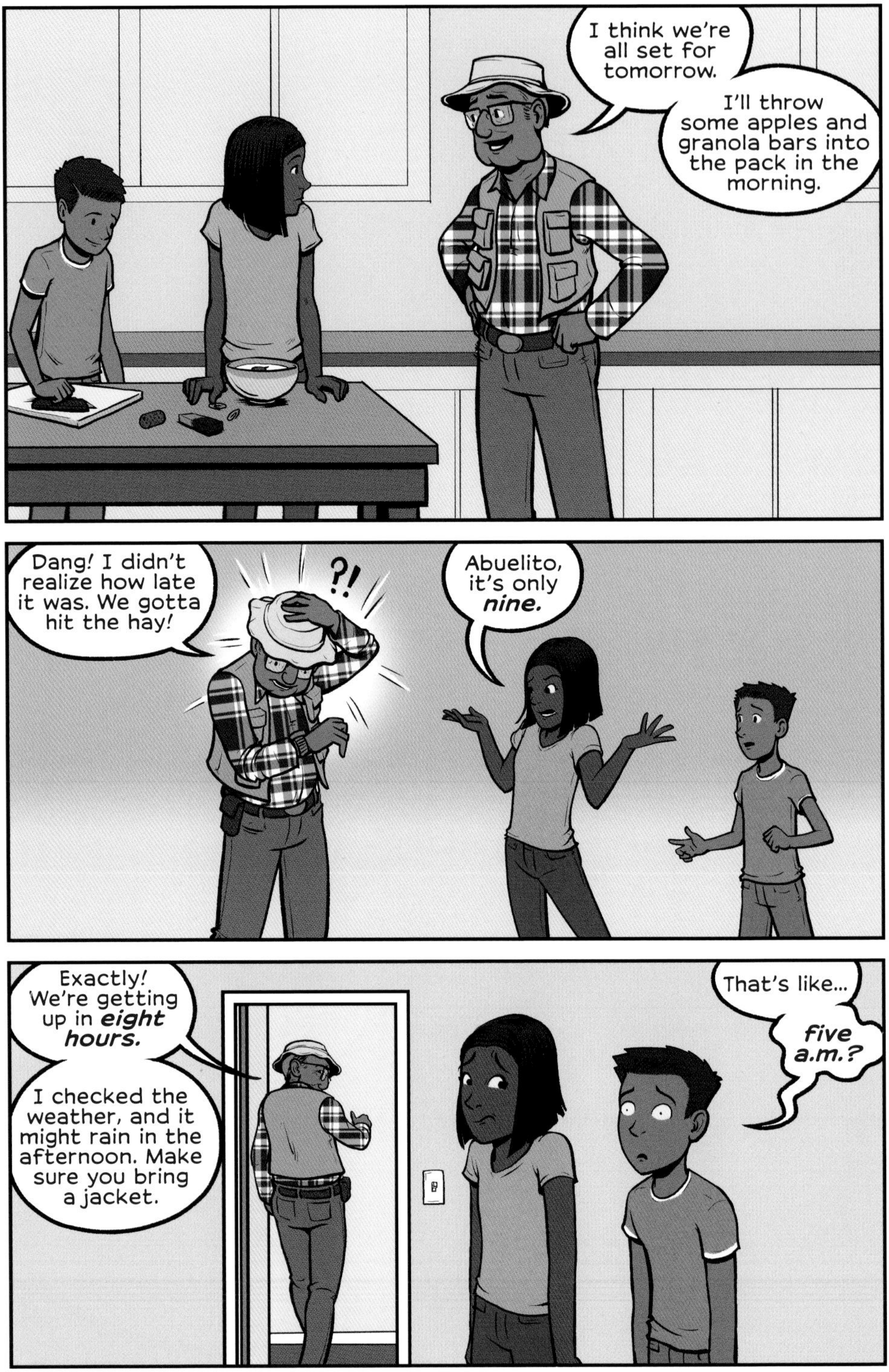
I think we're all set for tomorrow.
I'll throw some apples and granola bars into the pack in the morning.
Dang! I didn't realize how late it was. We gotta hit the hay!
?!
Abuelito, it's only *nine.*
Exactly! We're getting up in *eight hours.*
I checked the weather, and it might rain in the afternoon. Make sure you bring a jacket.
That's like...
*five a.m.?*

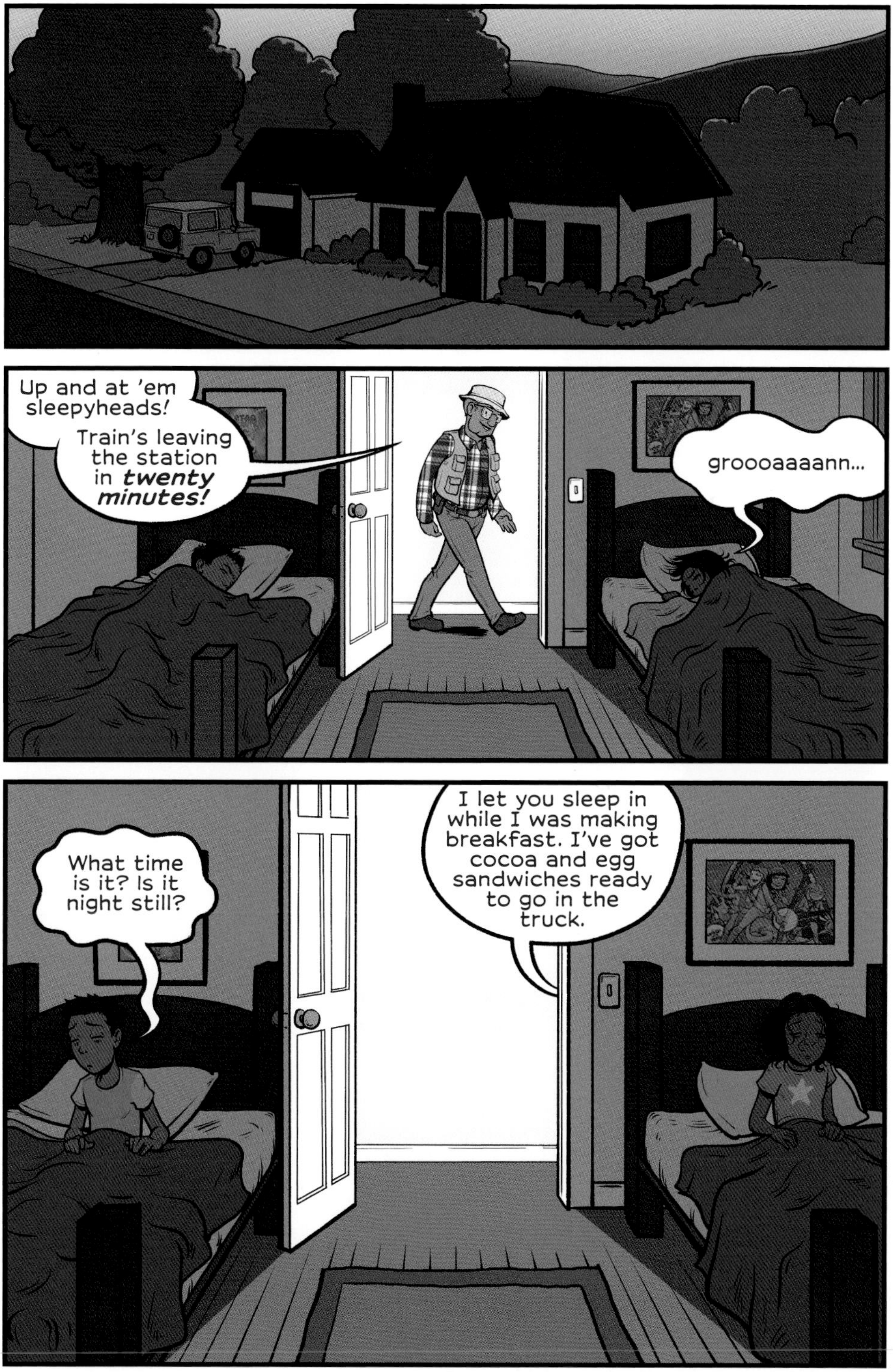
Up and at 'em sleepyheads!
Train's leaving the station in ***twenty minutes!***
groooaaaann...
What time is it? Is it night still?
I let you sleep in while I was making breakfast. I've got cocoa and egg sandwiches ready to go in the truck.

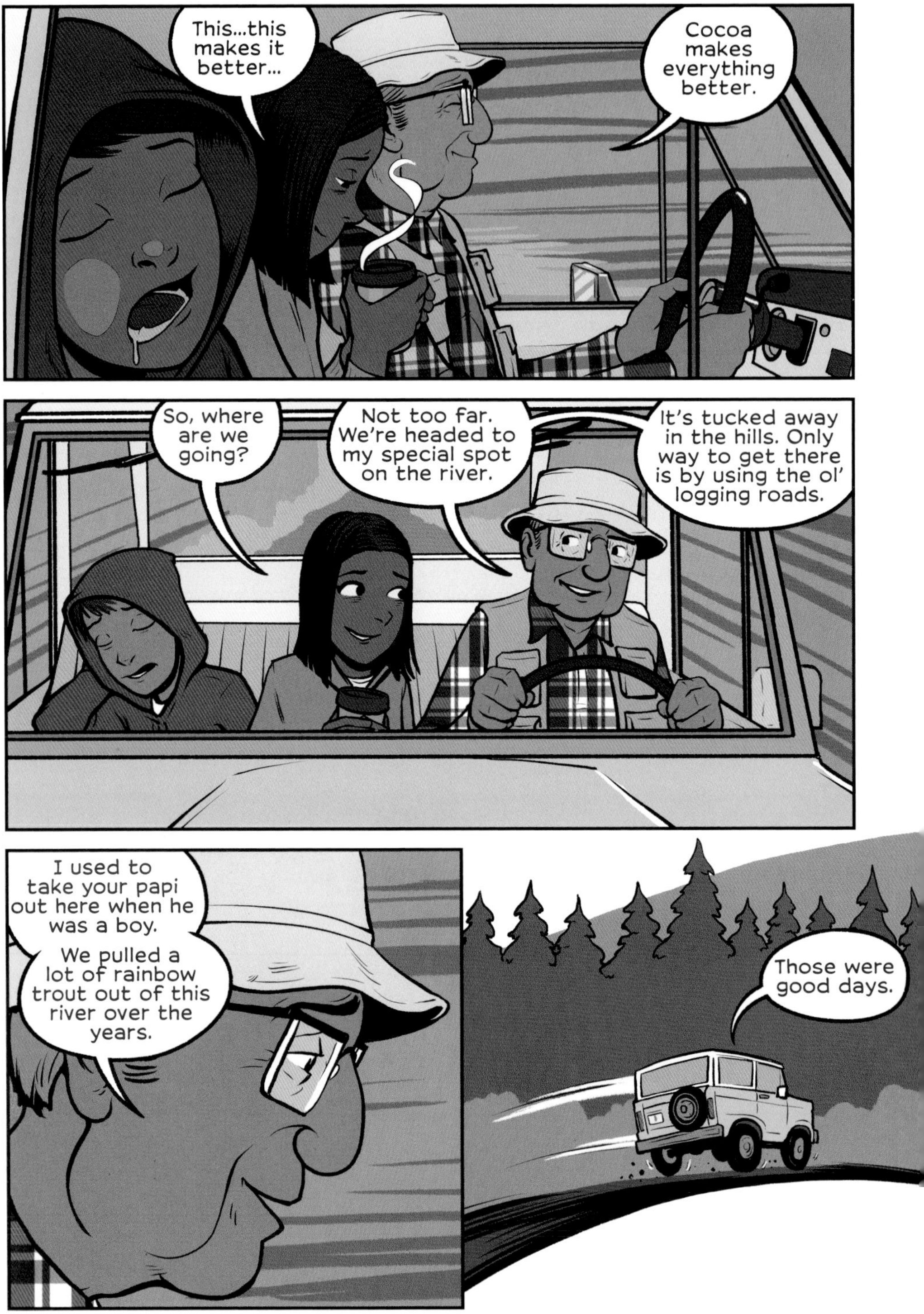

This...this makes it better...
Cocoa makes everything better.
So, where are we going?
Not too far. We're headed to my special spot on the river.
It's tucked away in the hills. Only way to get there is by using the ol' logging roads.
I used to take your papi out here when he was a boy.
We pulled a lot of rainbow trout out of this river over the years.
Those were good days.

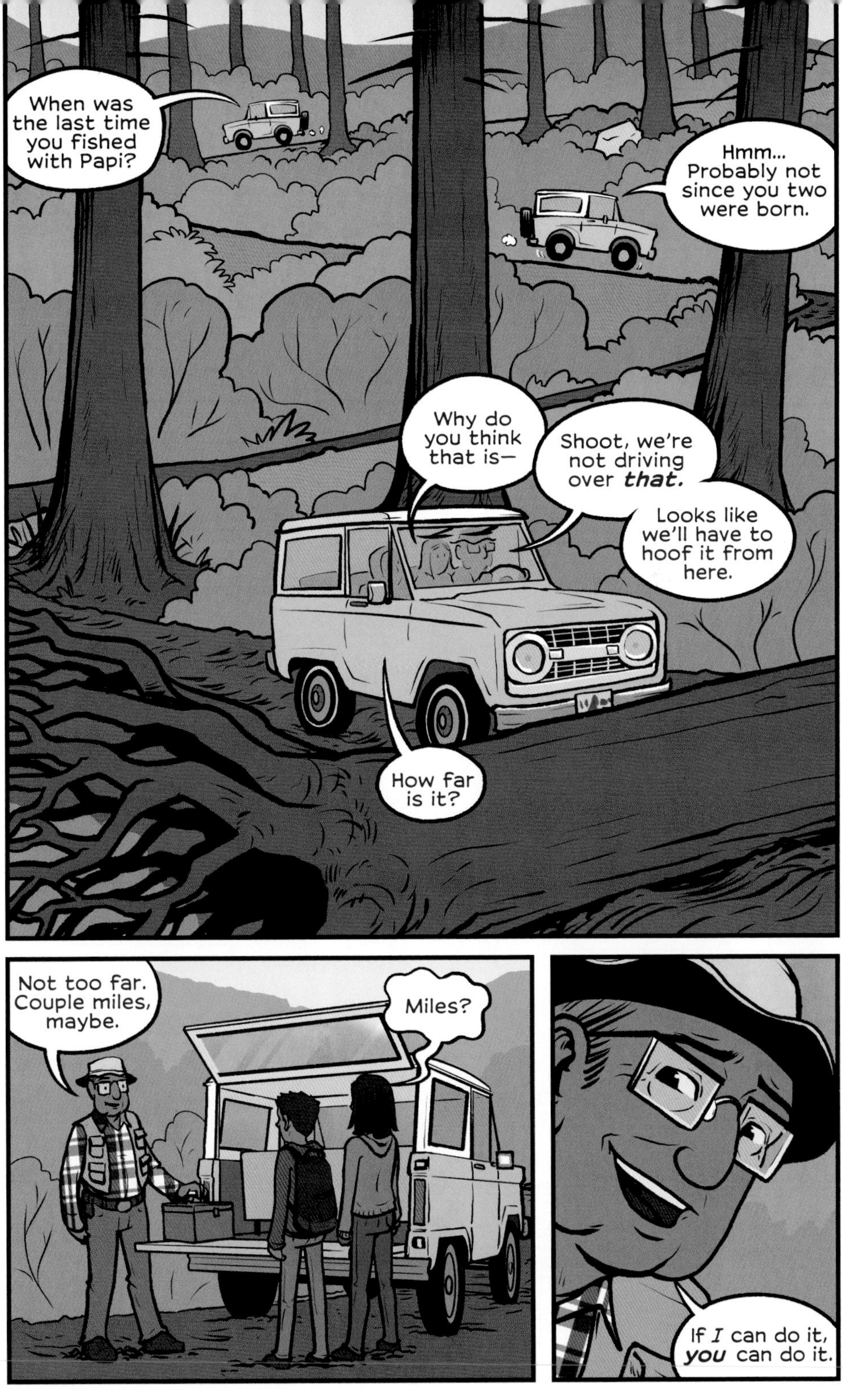
When was the last time you fished with Papi?
Hmm... Probably not since you two were born.
Why do you think that is—
Shoot, we're not driving over ***that.***
Looks like we'll have to hoof it from here.
How far is it?
Not too far. Couple miles, maybe.
Miles?
If *I* can do it, ***you*** can do it.

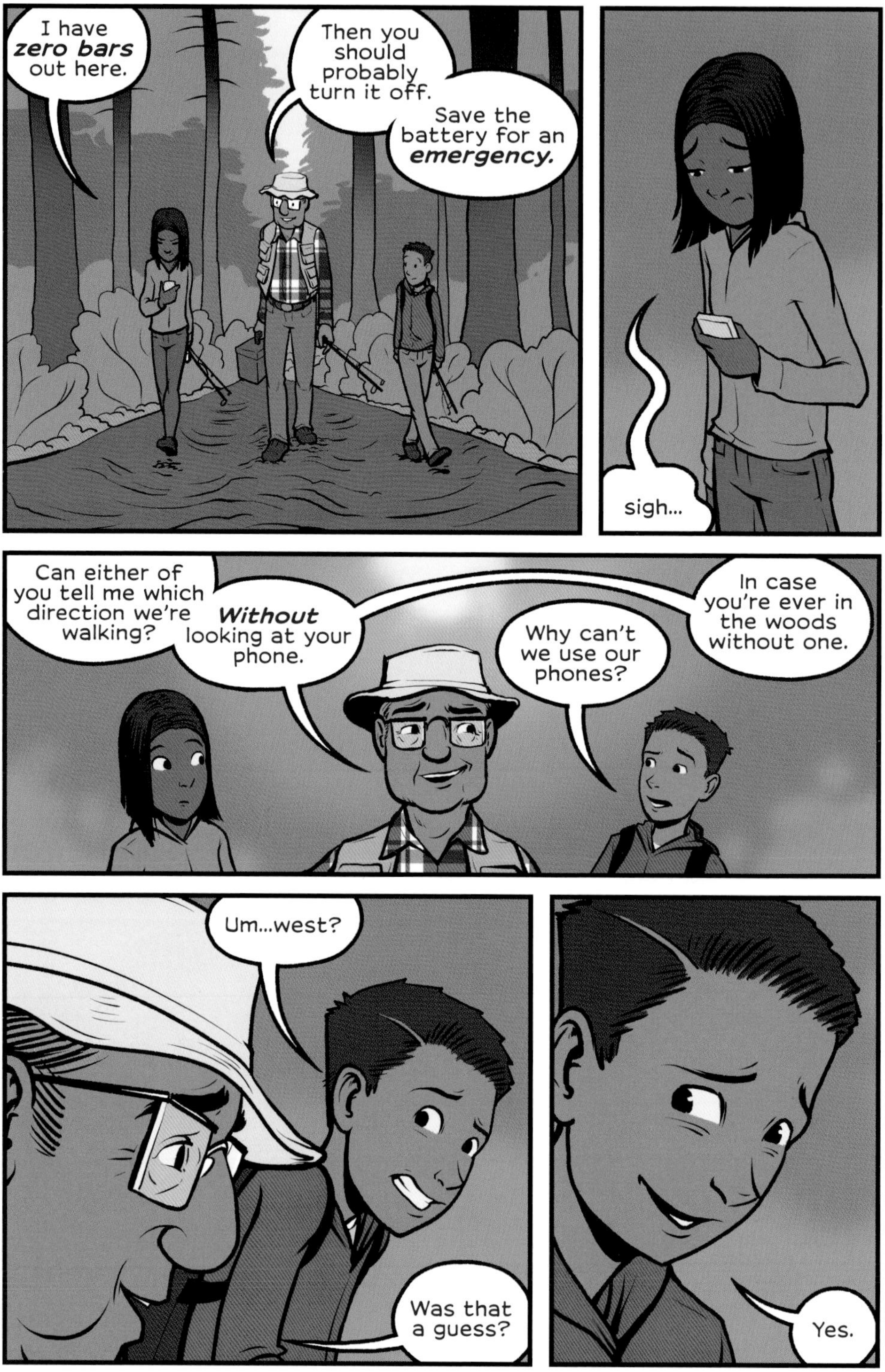
I have *zero bars* out here.
Then you should probably turn it off.
Save the battery for an *emergency.*
sigh...
Can either of you tell me which direction we're walking?
*Without* looking at your phone.
Why can't we use our phones?
In case you're ever in the woods without one.
Um...west?
Was that a guess?
Yes.

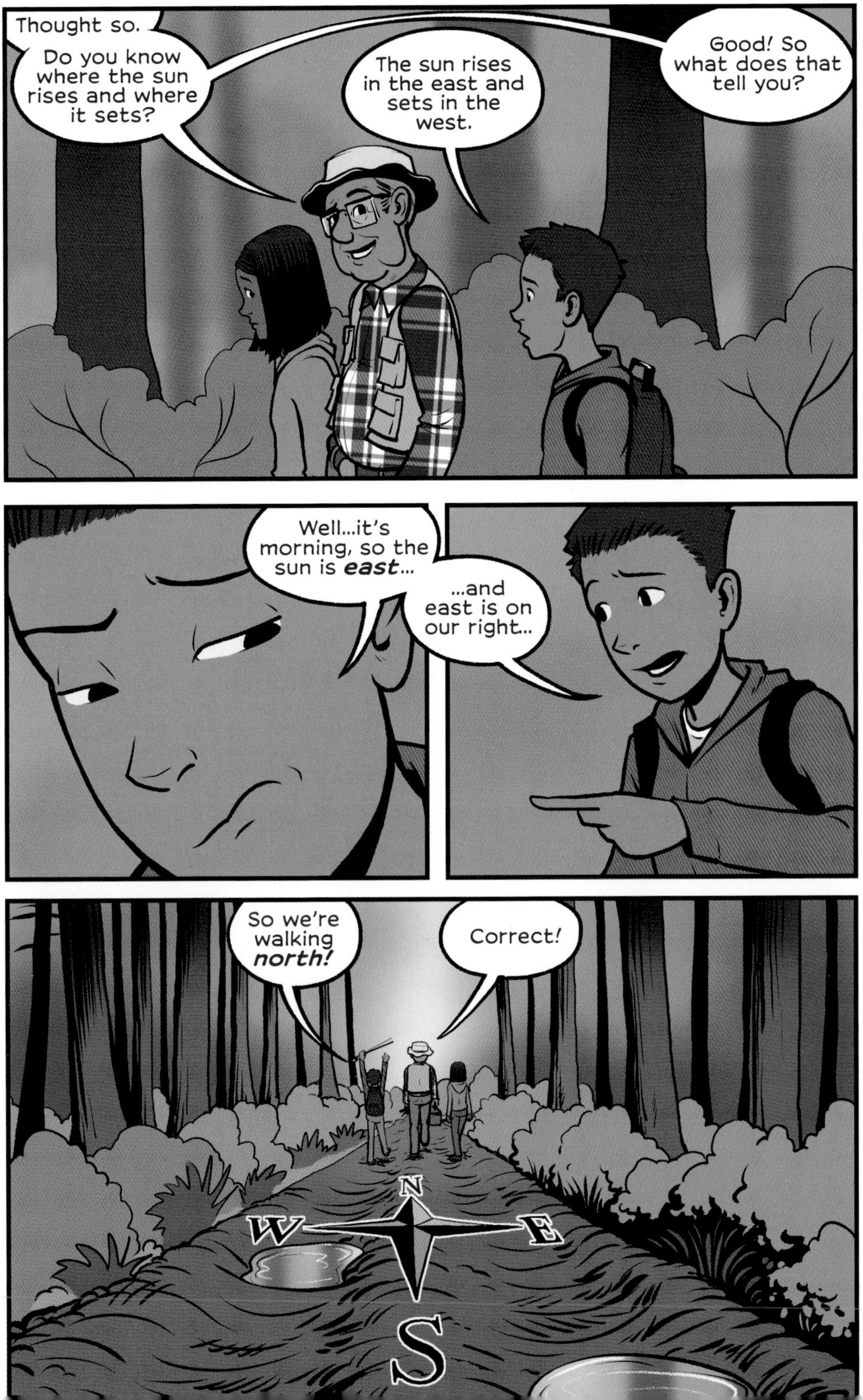
Thought so.
Do you know where the sun rises and where it sets?
The sun rises in the east and sets in the west.
Good! So what does that tell you?
Well...it's morning, so the sun is ***east***...
...and east is on our right...
So we're walking ***north!***
Correct!
N
W
E
S

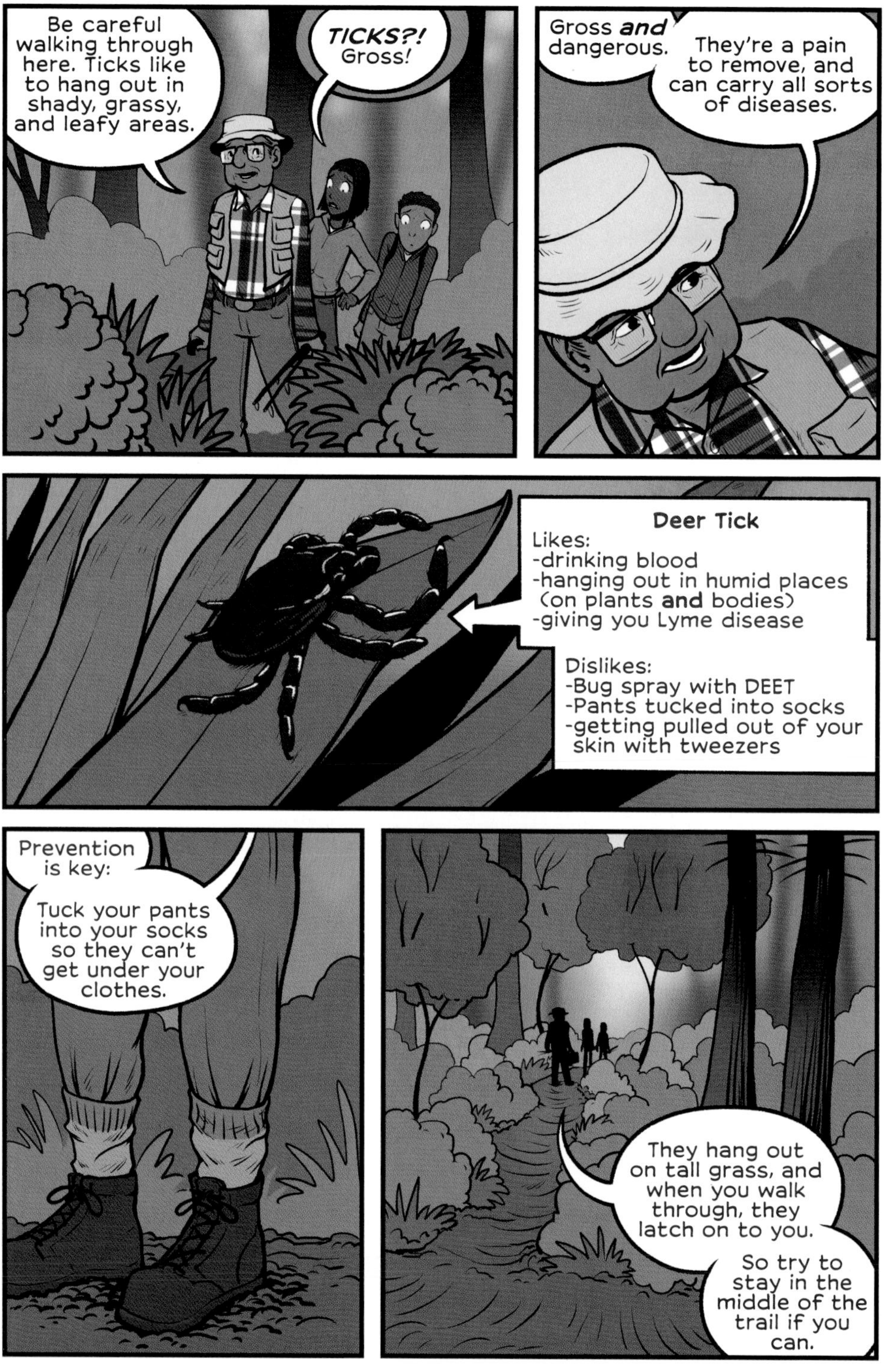
Be careful walking through here. Ticks like to hang out in shady, grassy, and leafy areas.
TICKS?! Gross!
Gross and dangerous.
They're a pain to remove, and can carry all sorts of diseases.
Deer Tick
Likes:
-drinking blood
-hanging out in humid places (on plants and bodies)
-giving you Lyme disease
Dislikes:
-Bug spray with DEET
-Pants tucked into socks
-getting pulled out of your skin with tweezers
Prevention is key:
Tuck your pants into your socks so they can't get under your clothes.
They hang out on tall grass, and when you walk through, they latch on to you.
So try to stay in the middle of the trail if you can.

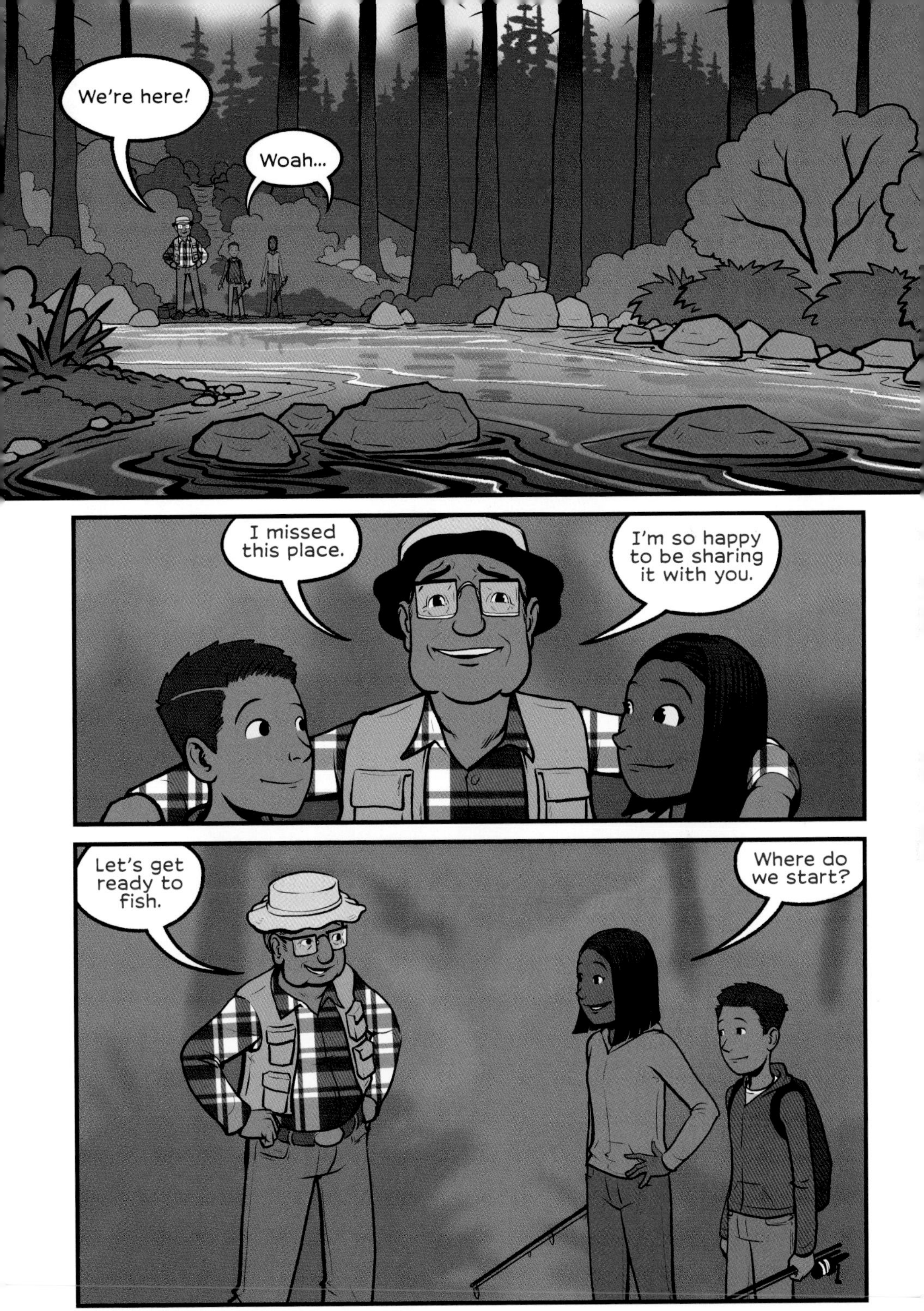
We're here!
Woah...
I missed this place.
I'm so happy to be sharing it with you.
Let's get ready to fish.
Where do we start?

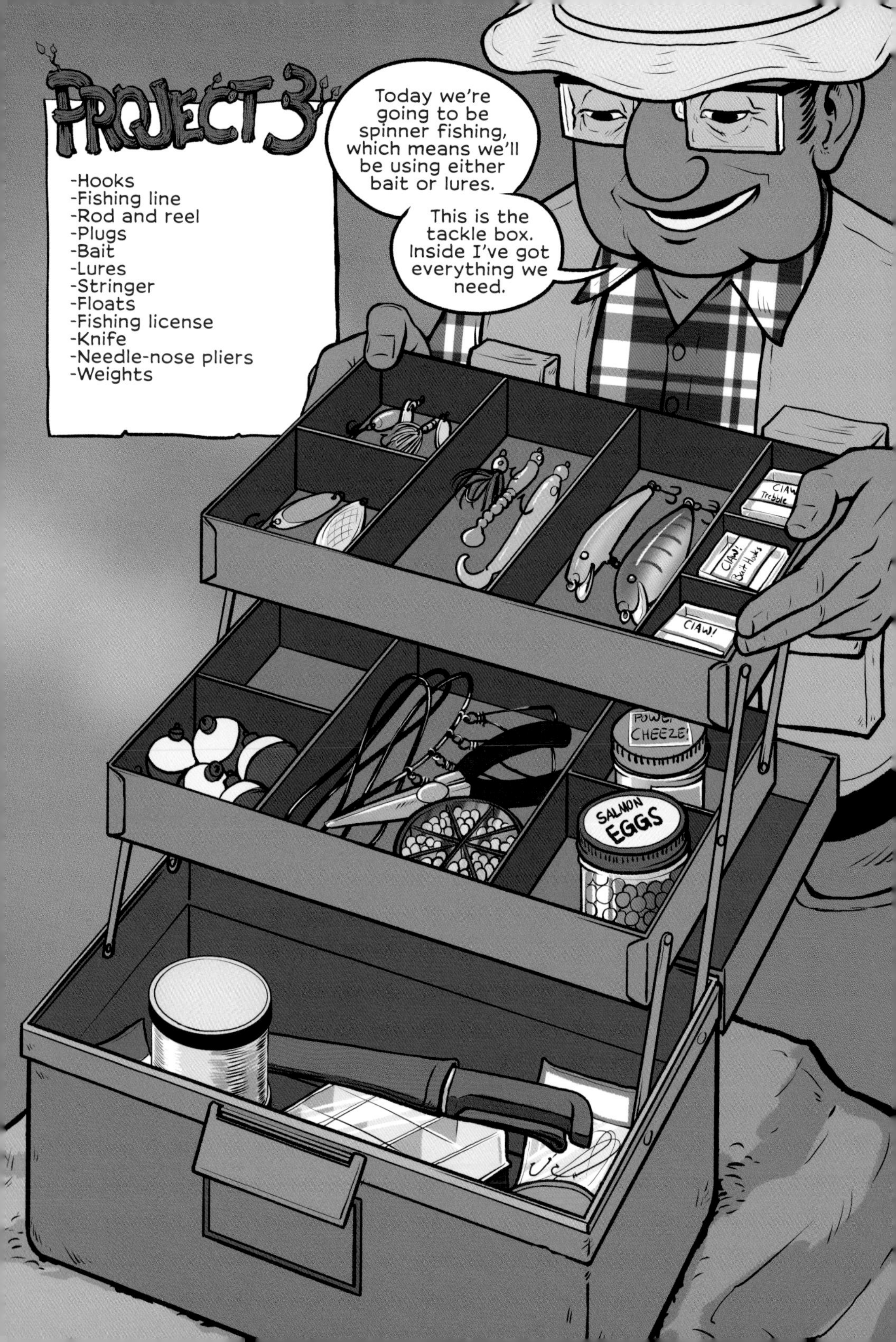
PROJECT 3
-Hooks
-Fishing line
-Rod and reel
-Plugs
-Bait
-Lures
-Stringer
-Floats
-Fishing license
-Knife
-Needle-nose pliers
-Weights
Today we're going to be spinner fishing, which means we'll be using either bait or lures.
This is the tackle box. Inside I've got everything we need.
CLAW! Trebble
CLAW! Bait Hooks
CLAW!
CHEEZE!
SALMON EGGS

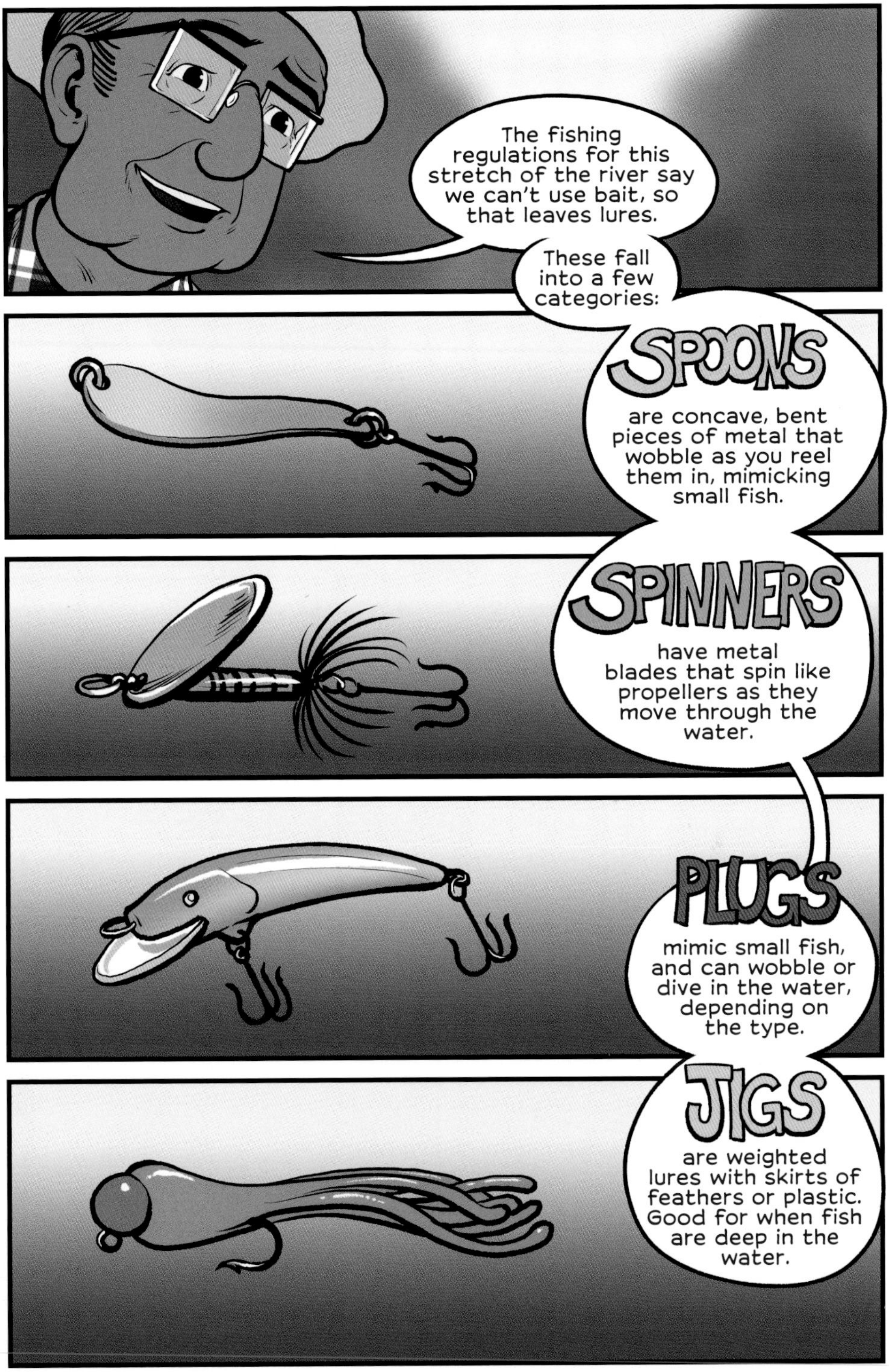

The fishing regulations for this stretch of the river say we can't use bait, so that leaves lures.
These fall into a few categories:
SPOONS
are concave, bent pieces of metal that wobble as you reel them in, mimicking small fish.
SPINNERS
have metal blades that spin like propellers as they move through the water.
PLUGS
mimic small fish, and can wobble or dive in the water, depending on the type.
JIGS
are weighted lures with skirts of feathers or plastic. Good for when fish are deep in the water.

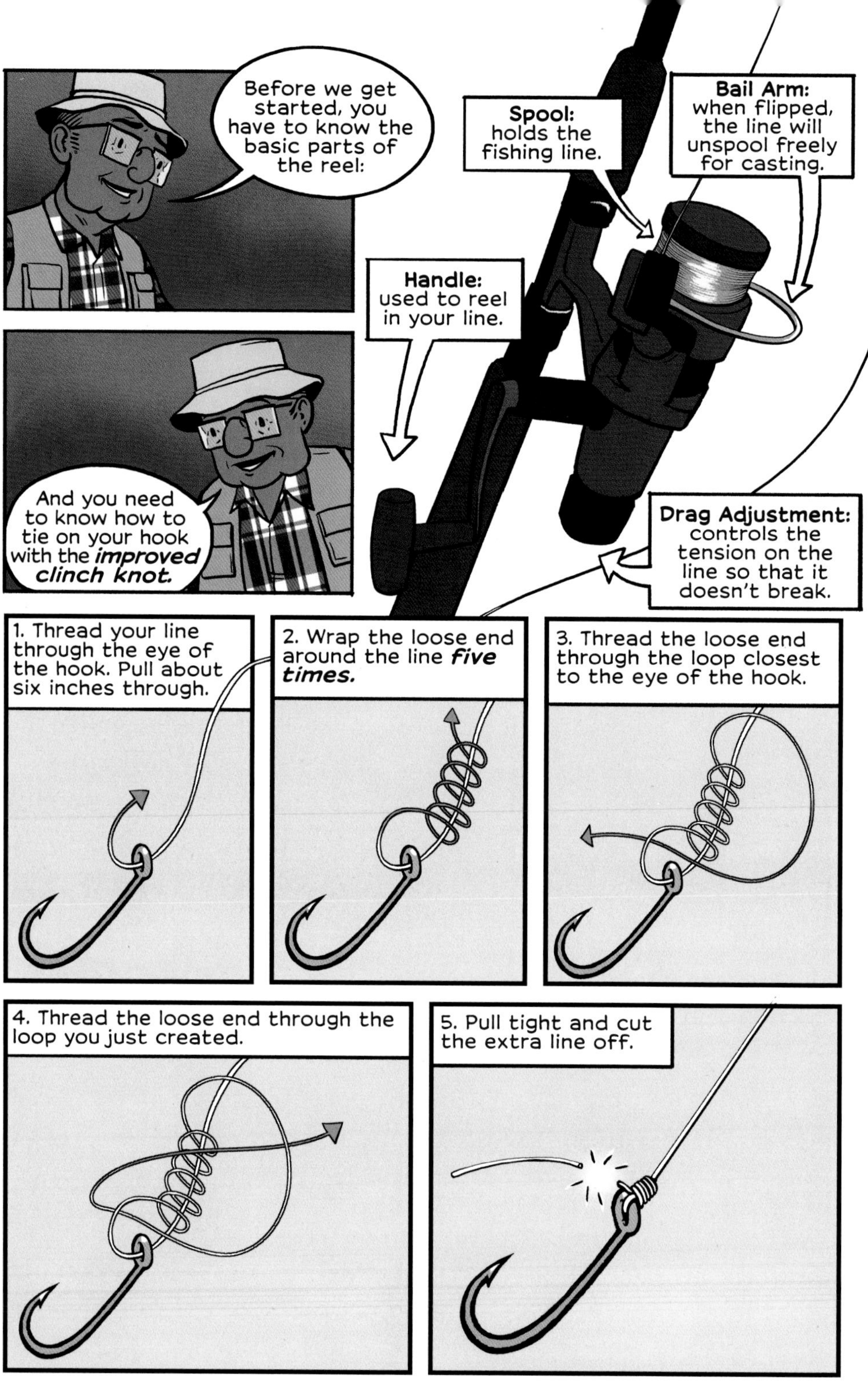
Before we get started, you have to know the basic parts of the reel:
Spool: holds the fishing line.
Bail Arm: when flipped, the line will unspool freely for casting.
Handle: used to reel in your line.
And you need to know how to tie on your hook with the *improved clinch knot.*
Drag Adjustment: controls the tension on the line so that it doesn't break.
1. Thread your line through the eye of the hook. Pull about six inches through.
2. Wrap the loose end around the line *five times.*
3. Thread the loose end through the loop closest to the eye of the hook.
4. Thread the loose end through the loop you just created.
5. Pull tight and cut the extra line off.

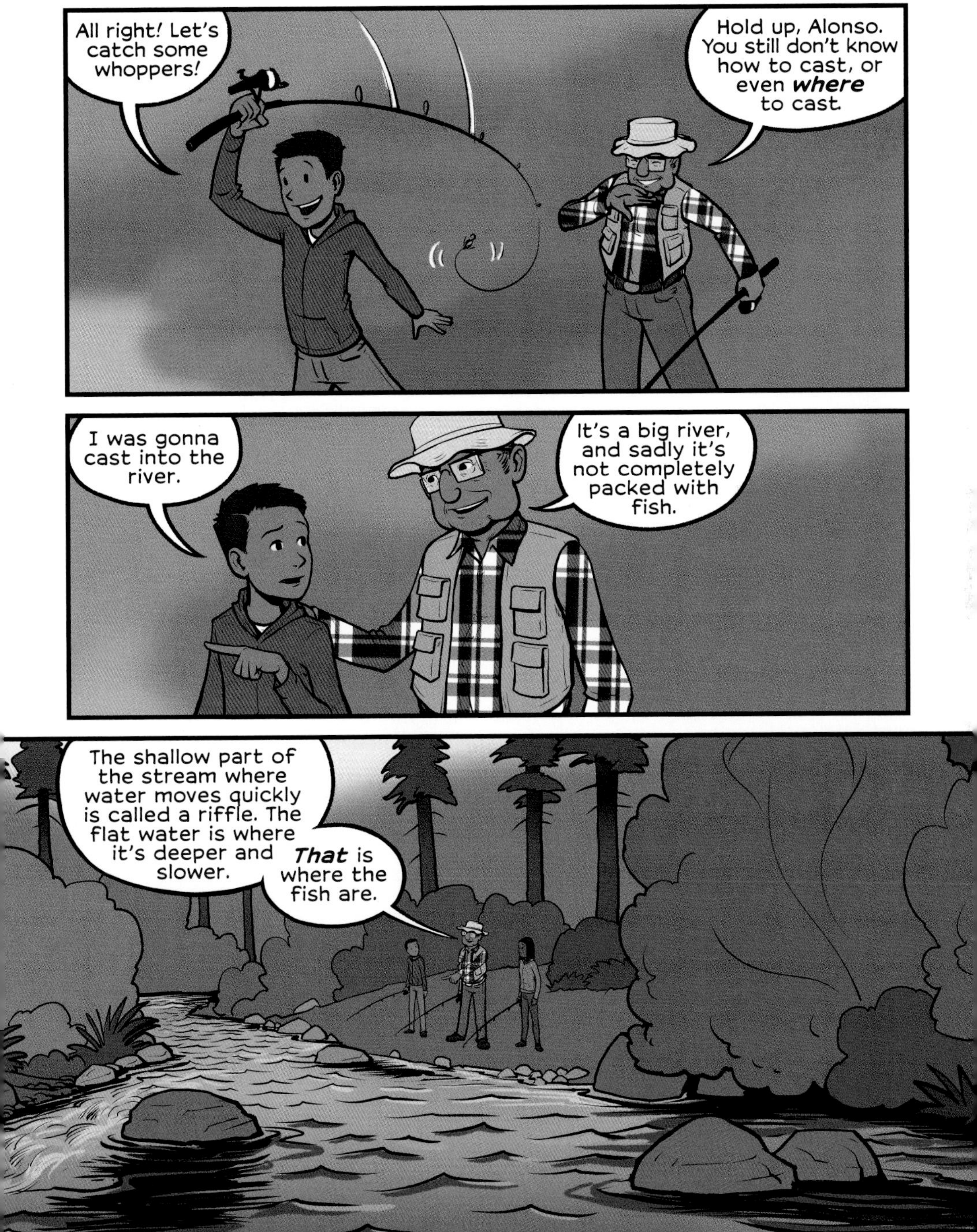
All right! Let's catch some whoppers!
Hold up, Alonso. You still don't know how to cast, or even *where* to cast.
I was gonna cast into the river.
It's a big river, and sadly it's not completely packed with fish.
The shallow part of the stream where water moves quickly is called a riffle. The flat water is where it's deeper and slower.
*That* is where the fish are.

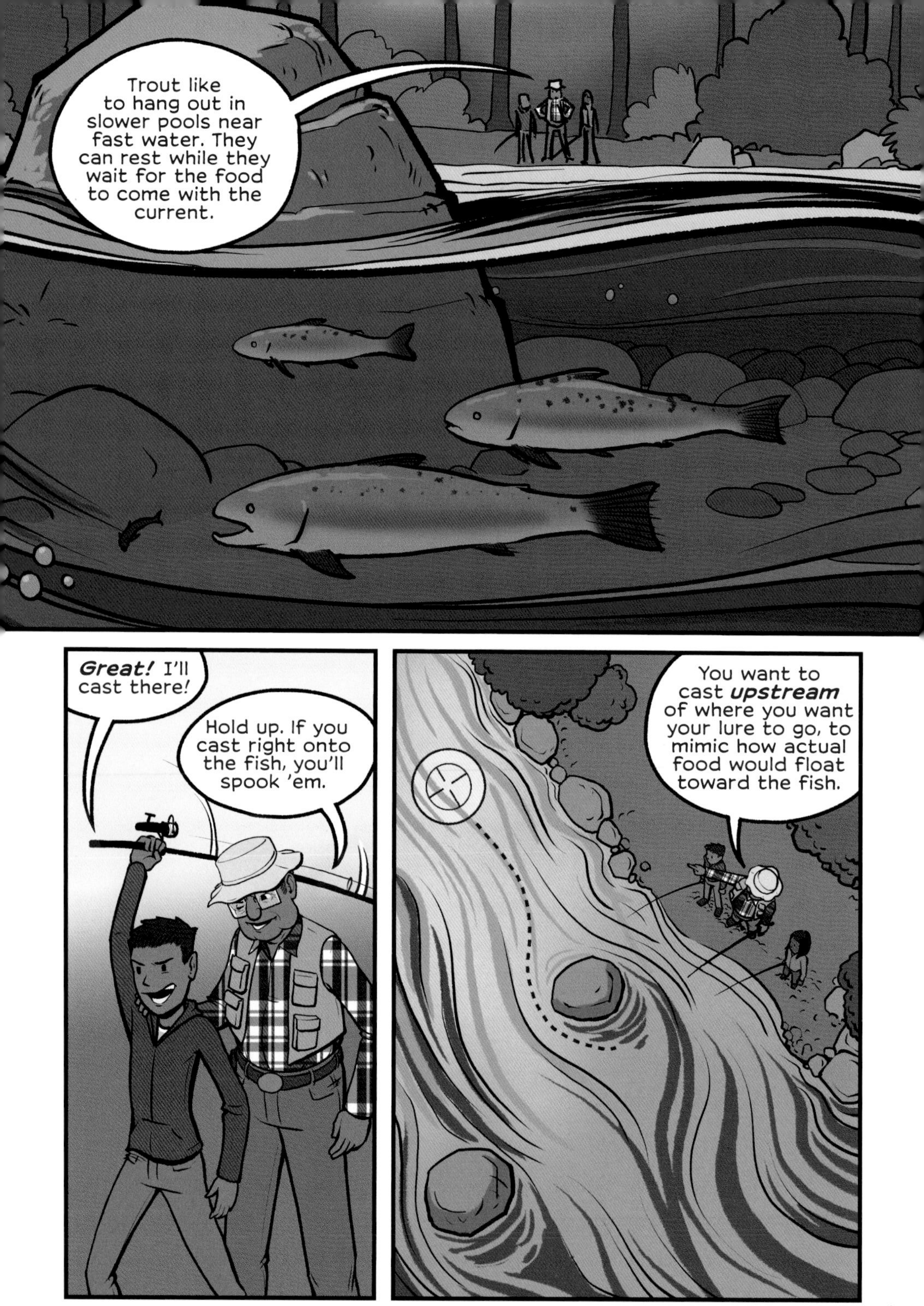

Trout like to hang out in slower pools near fast water. They can rest while they wait for the food to come with the current.
*Great!* I'll cast there!
Hold up. If you cast right onto the fish, you'll spook 'em.
You want to cast ***upstream*** of where you want your lure to go, to mimic how actual food would float toward the fish.

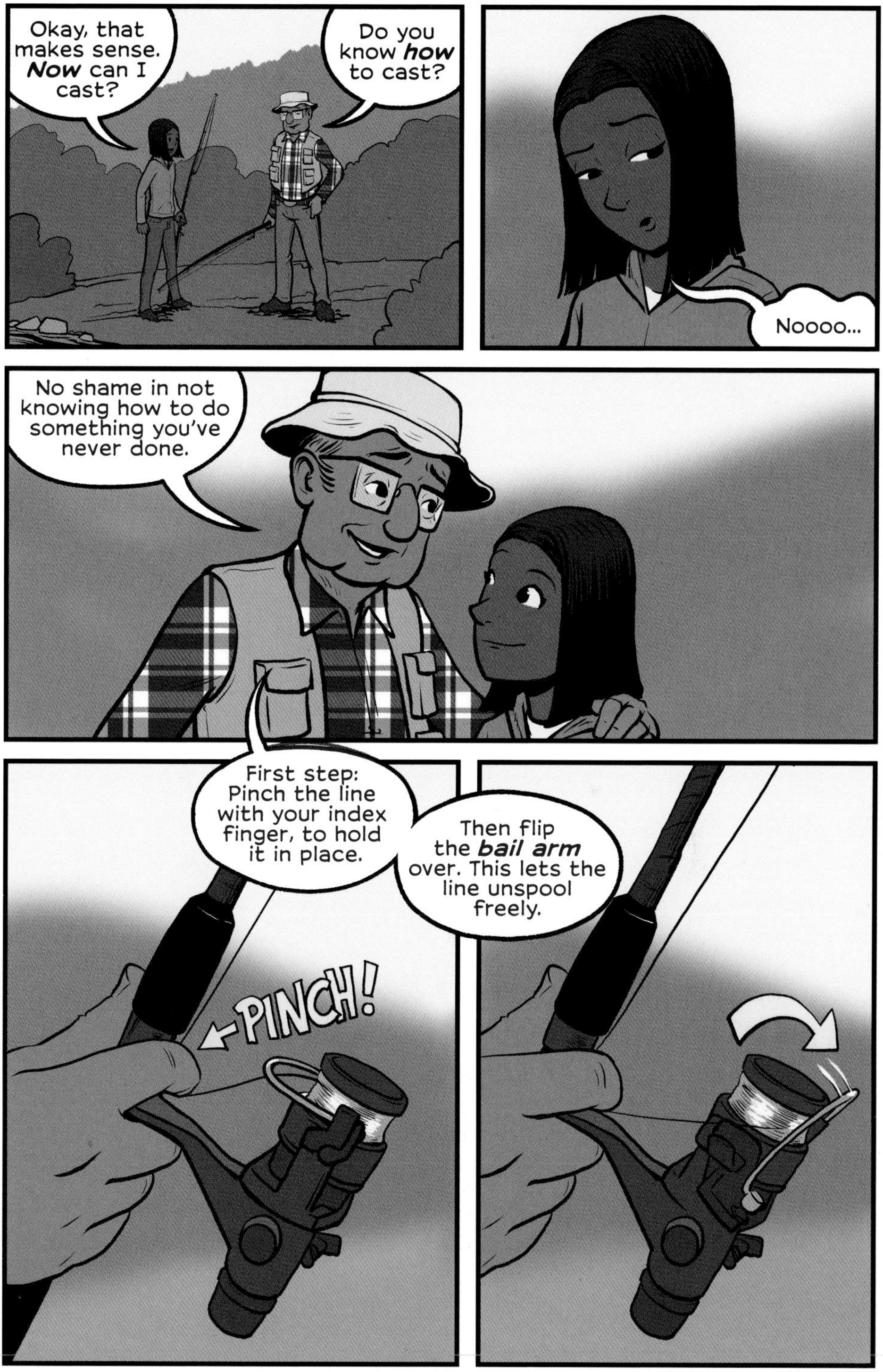
Okay, that makes sense. ***Now*** can I cast?
Do you know ***how*** to cast?
Noooo...
No shame in not knowing how to do something you've never done.
First step: Pinch the line with your index finger, to hold it in place.
PINCH!
Then flip the ***bail arm*** over. This lets the line unspool freely.

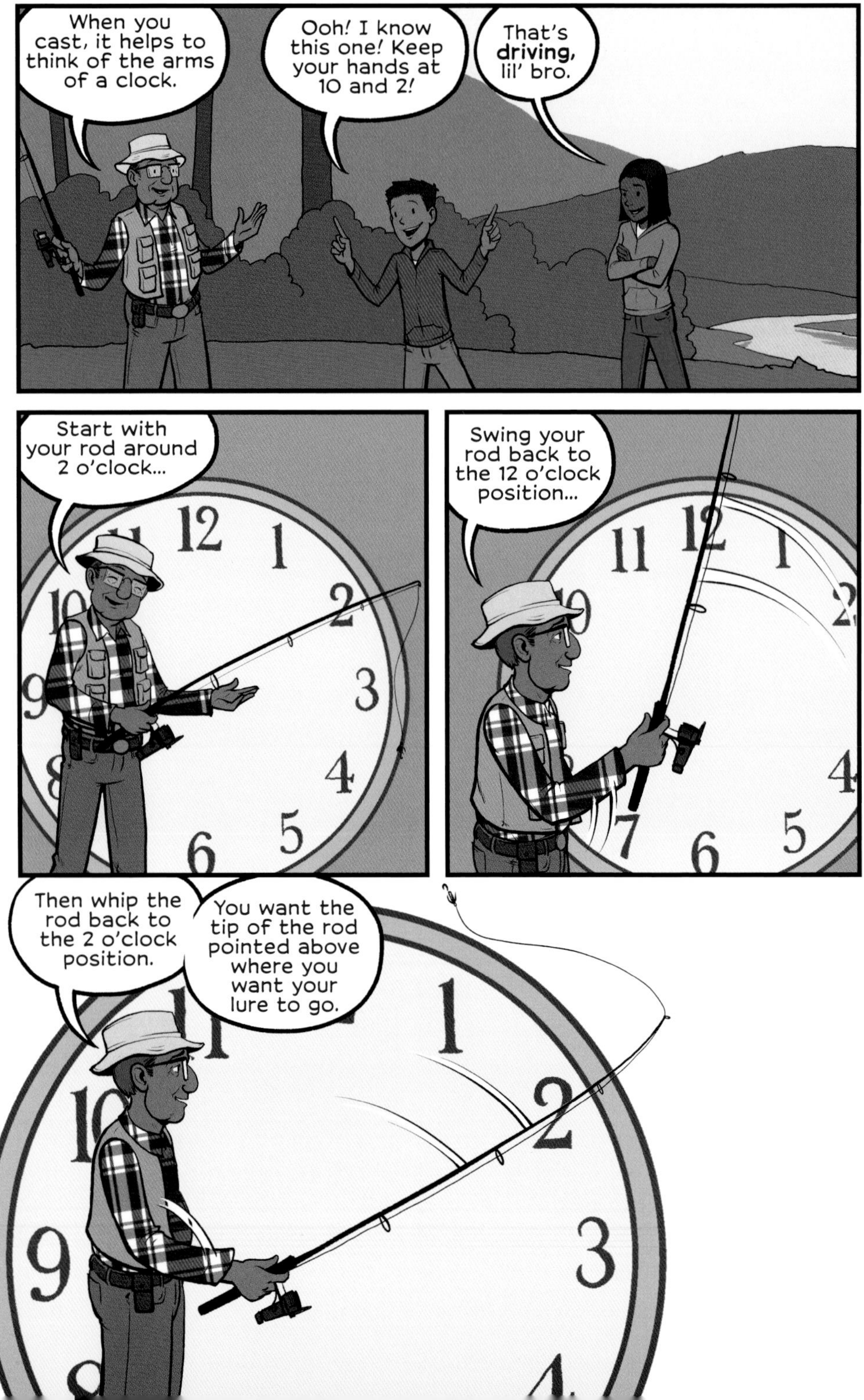
When you cast, it helps to think of the arms of a clock.
Ooh! I know this one! Keep your hands at 10 and 2!
That's **driving,** lil' bro.
Start with your rod around 2 o'clock...
Swing your rod back to the 12 o'clock position...
Then whip the rod back to the 2 o'clock position.
You want the tip of the rod pointed above where you want your lure to go.

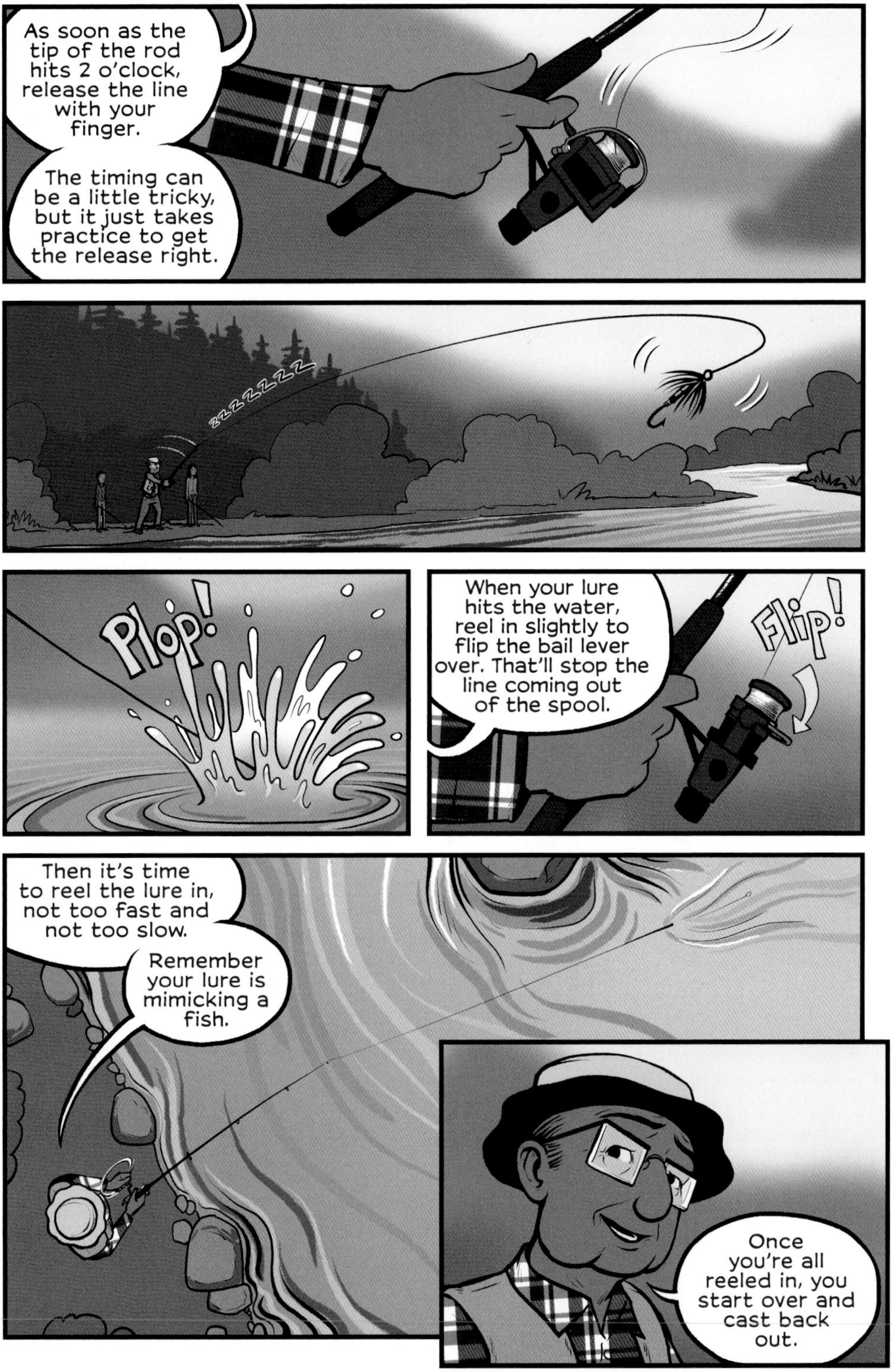
As soon as the tip of the rod hits 2 o'clock, release the line with your finger.
The timing can be a little tricky, but it just takes practice to get the release right.
zzzzzzz
Plop!
When your lure hits the water, reel in slightly to flip the bail lever over. That'll stop the line coming out of the spool.
Flip!
Then it's time to reel the lure in, not too fast and not too slow.
Remember your lure is mimicking a fish.
Once you're all reeled in, you start over and cast back out.

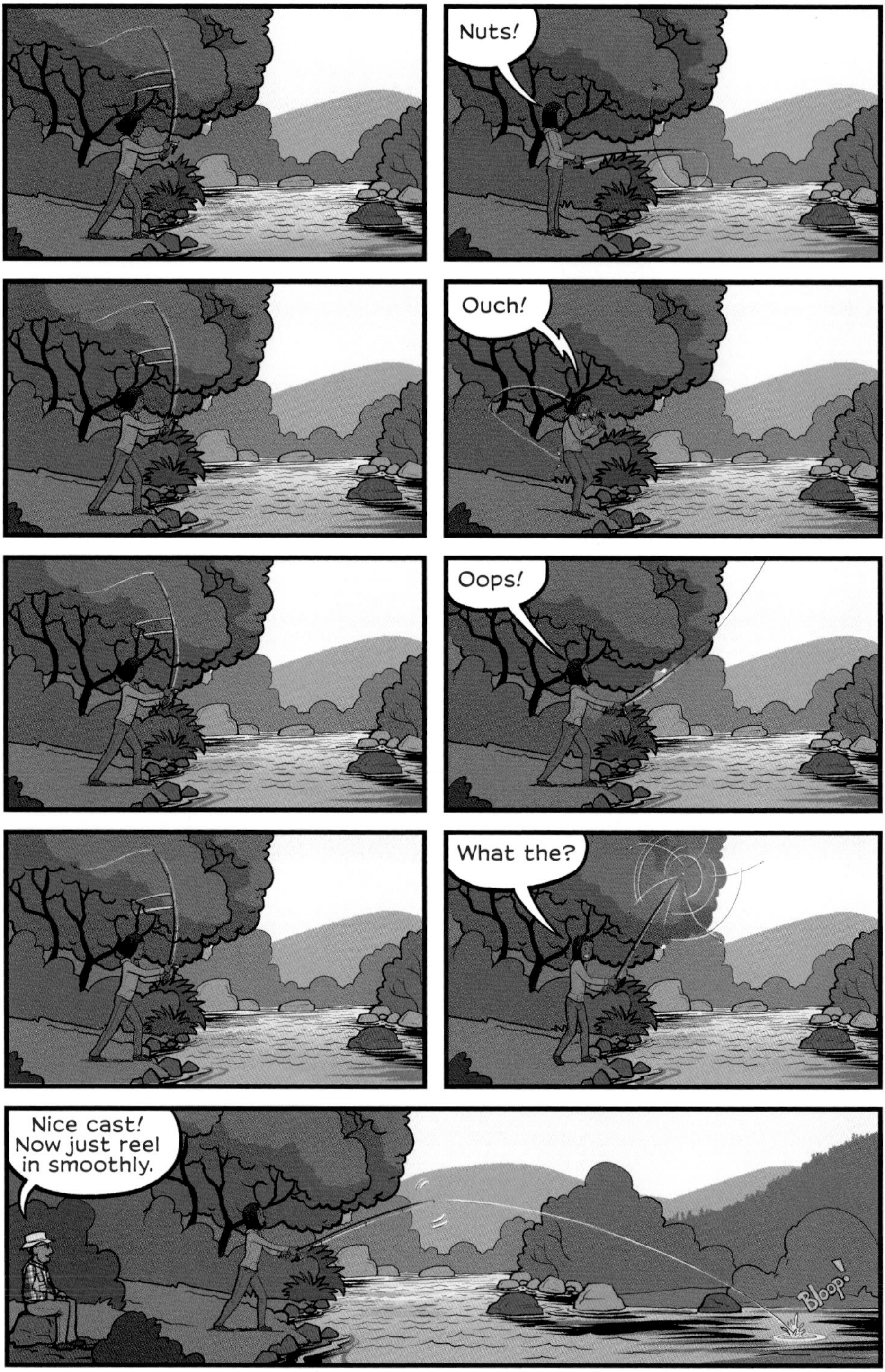
Nuts!
Ouch!
Oops!
What the?
Nice cast! Now just reel in smoothly.
Bloop!

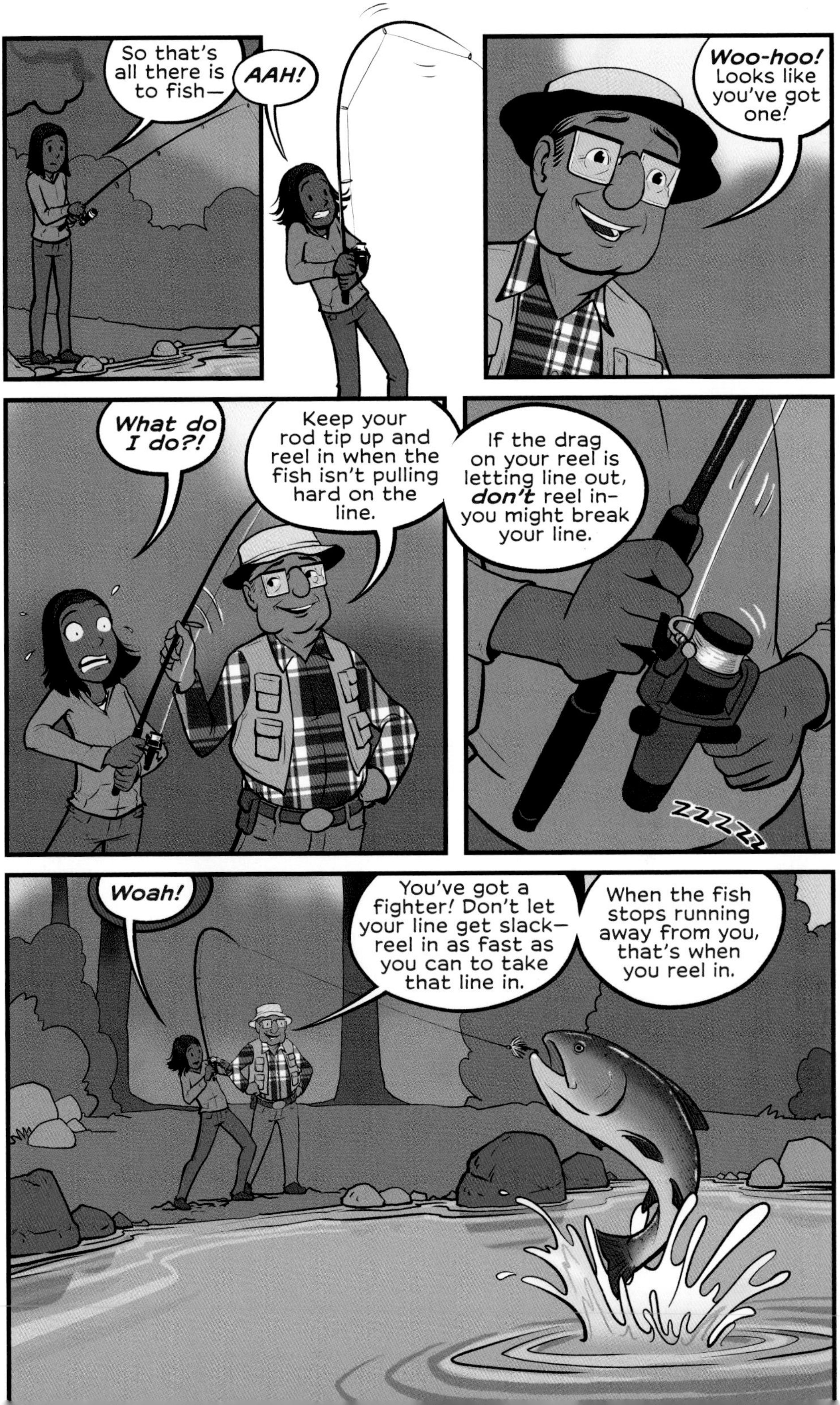
So that's all there is to fish—
AAH!
Woo-hoo! Looks like you've got one!
What do I do?!
Keep your rod tip up and reel in when the fish isn't pulling hard on the line.
If the drag on your reel is letting line out, don't reel in–you might break your line.
ZZZZZ
Woah!
You've got a fighter! Don't let your line get slack–reel in as fast as you can to take that line in.
When the fish stops running away from you, that's when you reel in.

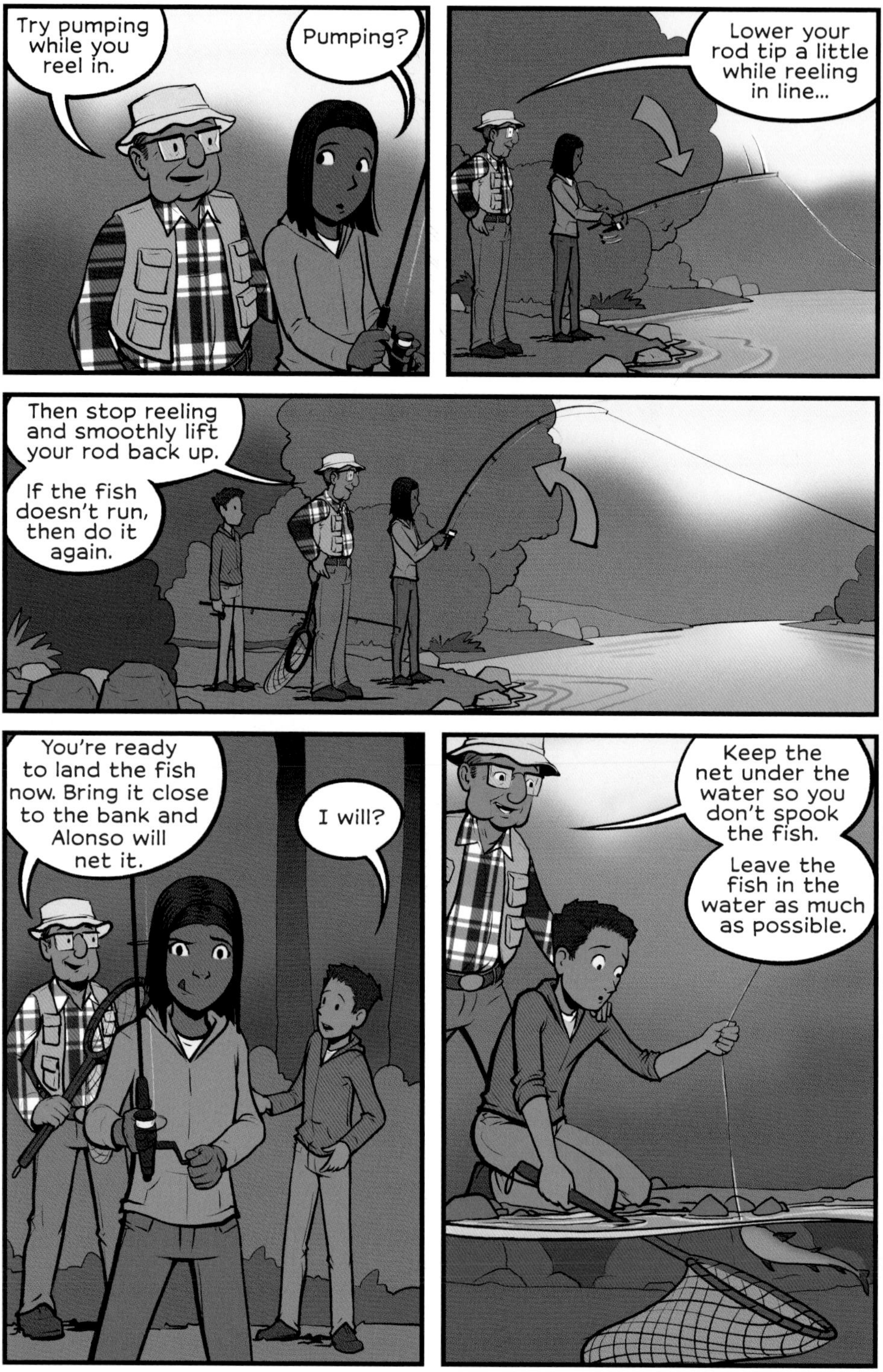
Try pumping while you reel in.
Pumping?
Lower your rod tip a little while reeling in line...
Then stop reeling and smoothly lift your rod back up.
If the fish doesn't run, then do it again.
You're ready to land the fish now. Bring it close to the bank and Alonso will net it.
I will?
Keep the net under the water so you don't spook the fish.
Leave the fish in the water as much as possible.

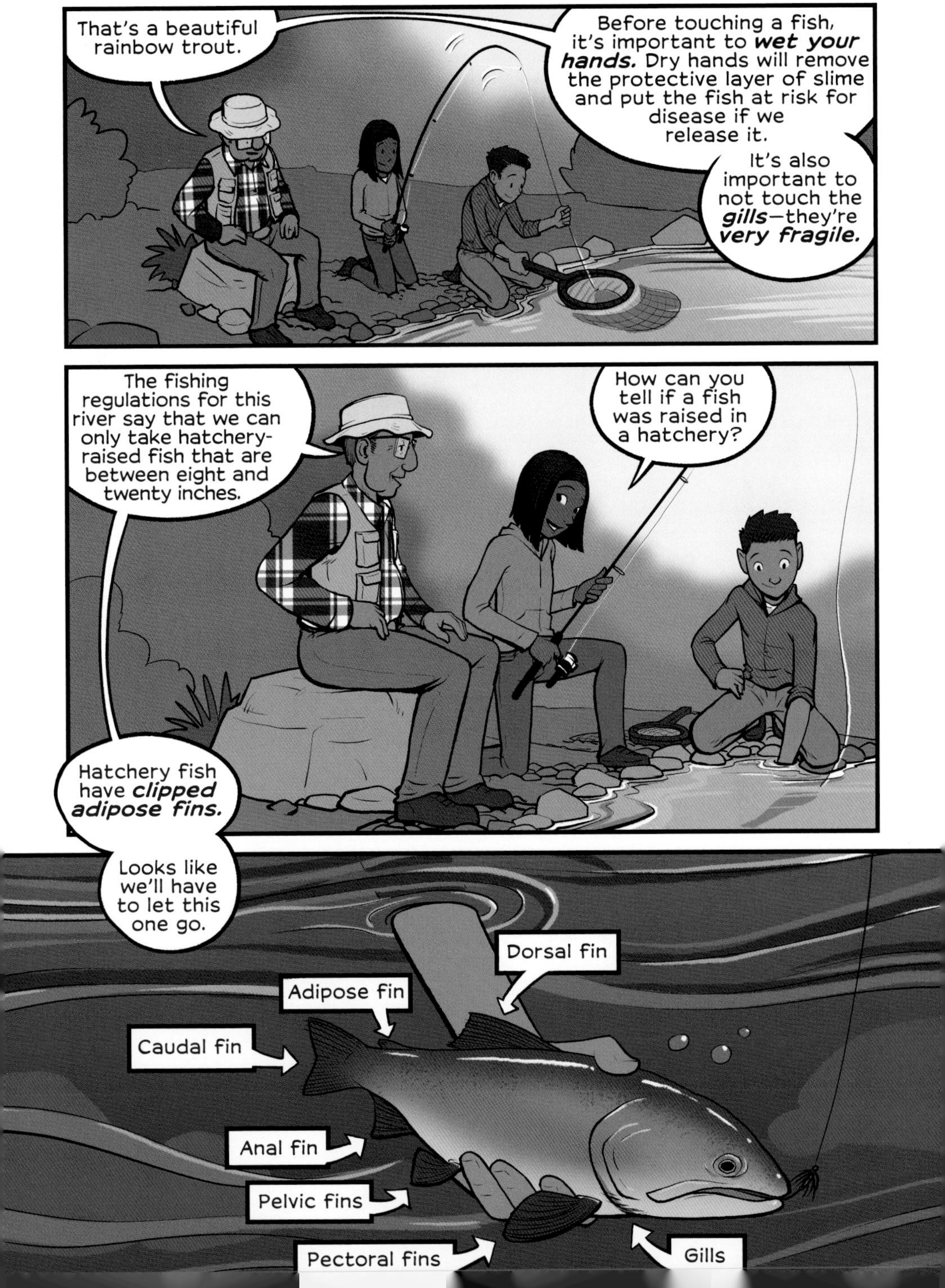
That's a beautiful rainbow trout.
Before touching a fish, it's important to ***wet your hands.*** Dry hands will remove the protective layer of slime and put the fish at risk for disease if we release it.
It's also important to not touch the ***gills***—they're ***very fragile.***
The fishing regulations for this river say that we can only take hatchery-raised fish that are between eight and twenty inches.
How can you tell if a fish was raised in a hatchery?
Hatchery fish have ***clipped adipose fins.***
Looks like we'll have to let this one go.
Dorsal fin
Adipose fin
Caudal fin
Anal fin
Pelvic fins
Pectoral fins
Gills

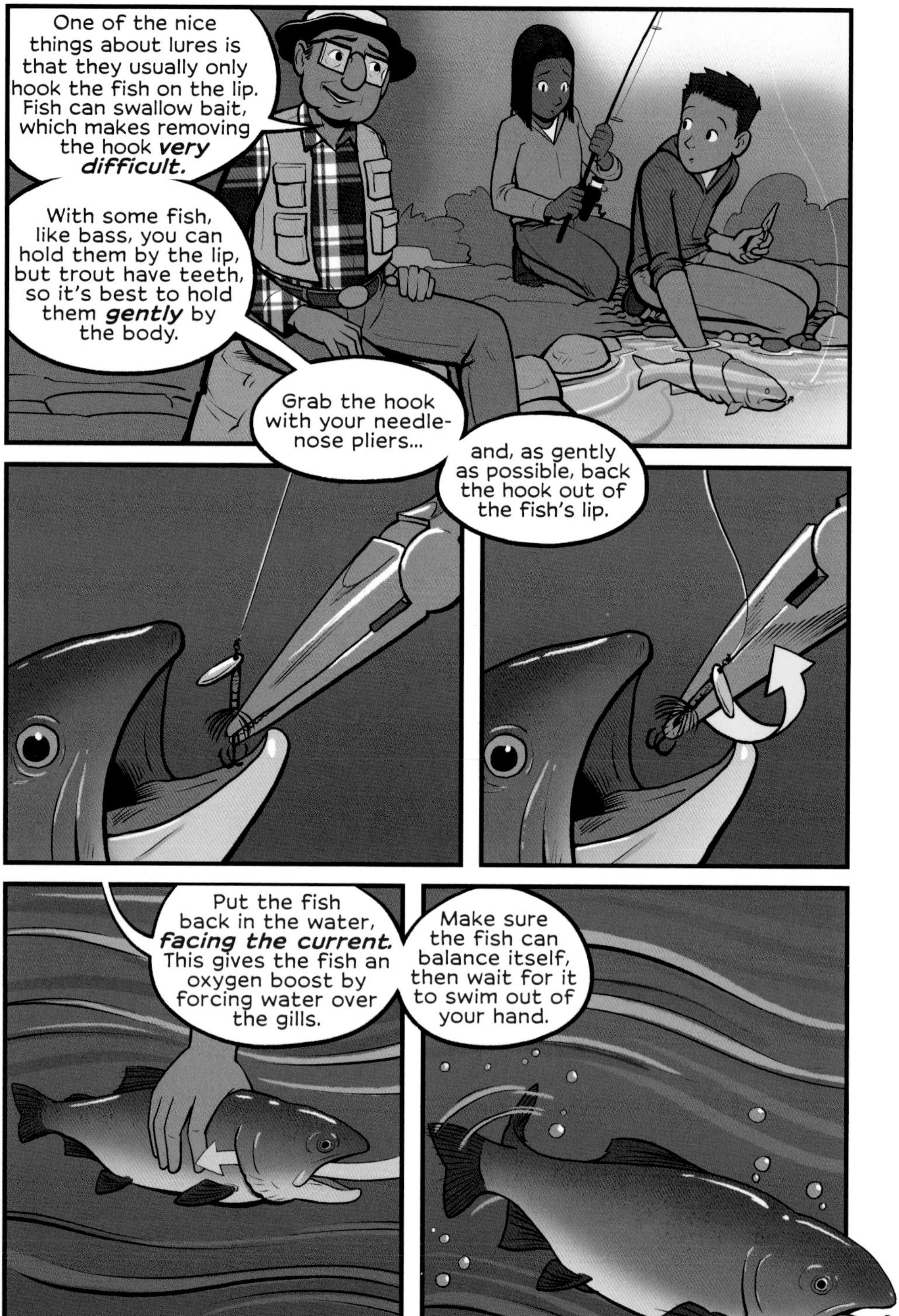
One of the nice things about lures is that they usually only hook the fish on the lip. Fish can swallow bait, which makes removing the hook ***very difficult.***
With some fish, like bass, you can hold them by the lip, but trout have teeth, so it's best to hold them ***gently*** by the body.
Grab the hook with your needle-nose pliers...
and, as gently as possible, back the hook out of the fish's lip.
Put the fish back in the water, ***facing the current.*** This gives the fish an oxygen boost by forcing water over the gills.
Make sure the fish can balance itself, then wait for it to swim out of your hand.

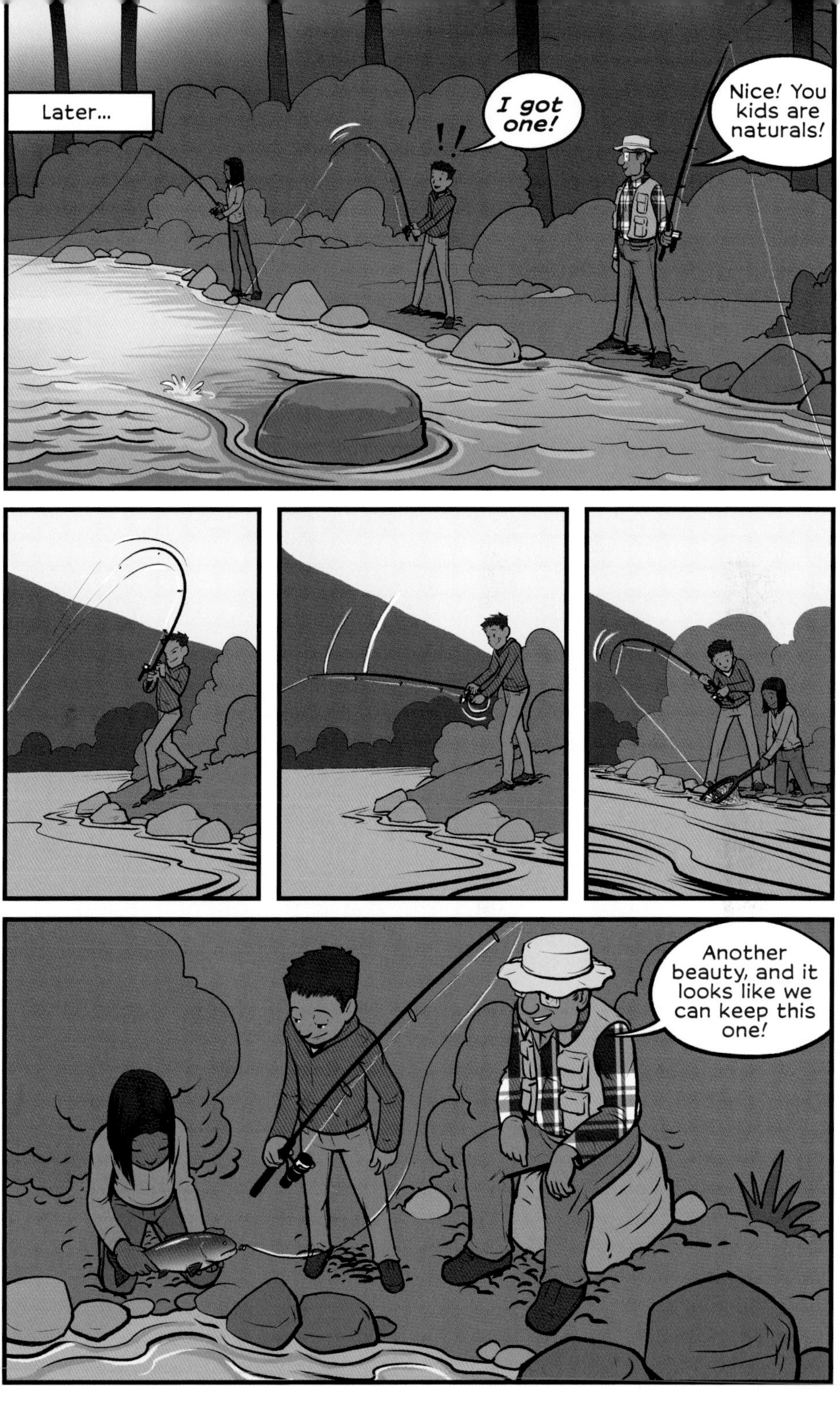
Later...
I got one!
! !
Nice! You kids are naturals!
Another beauty, and it looks like we can keep this one!

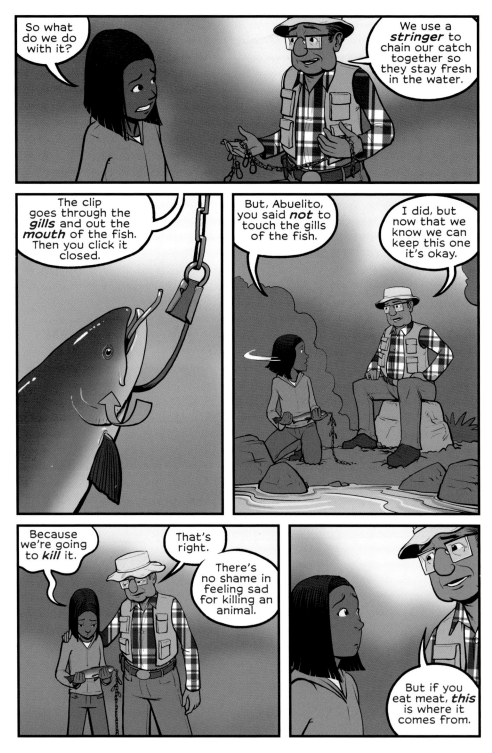

So what do we do with it?

We use a *stringer* to chain our catch together so they stay fresh in the water.

The clip goes through the *gills* and out the *mouth* of the fish. Then you click it closed.

But, Abuelito, you said *not* to touch the gills of the fish.

I did, but now that we know we can keep this one it's okay.

Because we're going to *kill* it.

That's right.

There's no shame in feeling sad for killing an animal.

But if you eat meat, *this* is where it comes from.

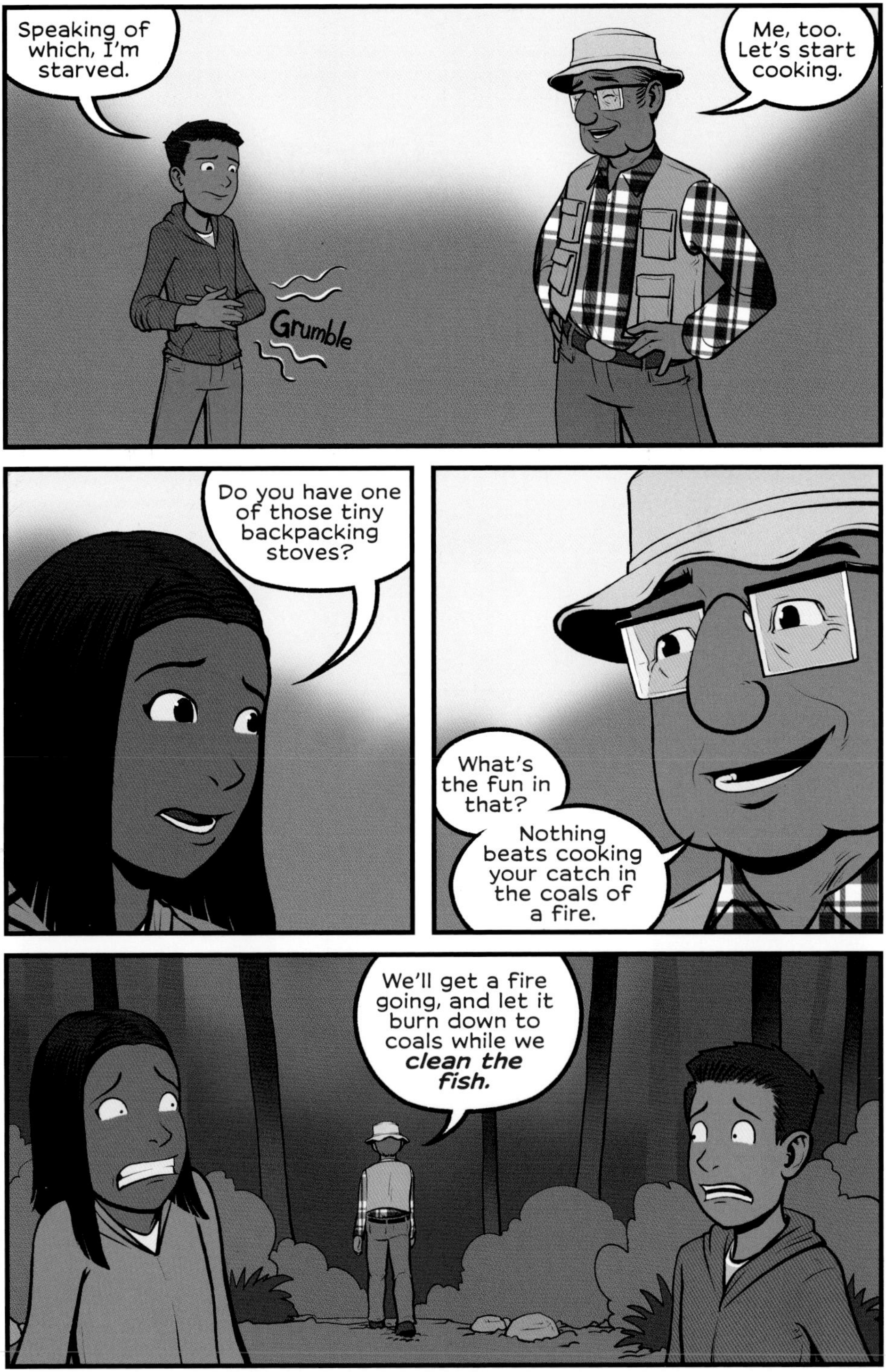
Speaking of which, I'm starved.
Me, too. Let's start cooking.
Grumble
Do you have one of those tiny backpacking stoves?
What's the fun in that?
Nothing beats cooking your catch in the coals of a fire.
We'll get a fire going, and let it burn down to coals while we ***clean the fish.***

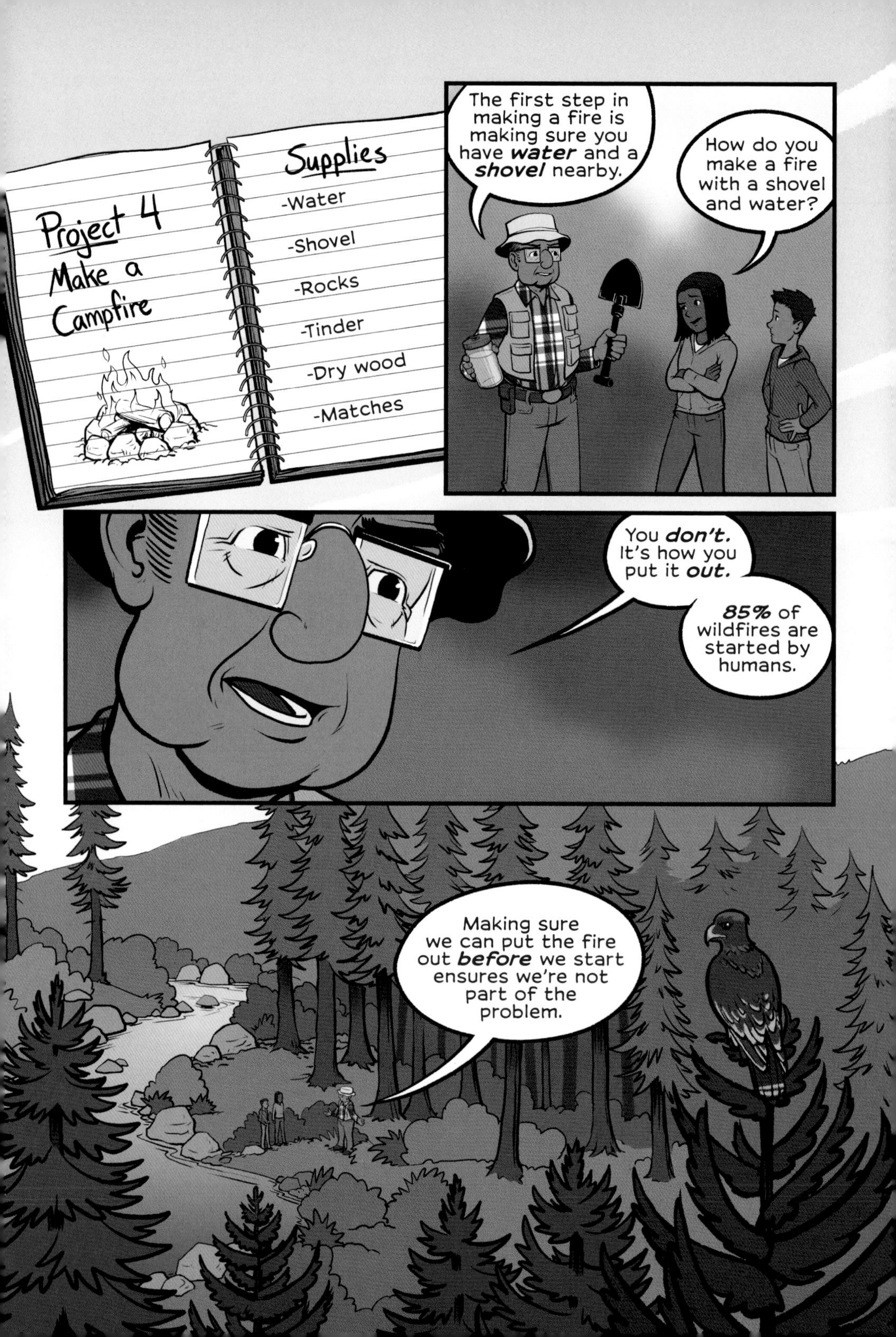

Project 4
Make a Campfire
Supplies
-Water
-Shovel
-Rocks
-Tinder
-Dry wood
-Matches
The first step in making a fire is making sure you have **water** and a **shovel** nearby.
How do you make a fire with a shovel and water?
You **don't.** It's how you put it **out.**
**85%** of wildfires are started by humans.
Making sure we can put the fire out **before** we start ensures we're not part of the problem.

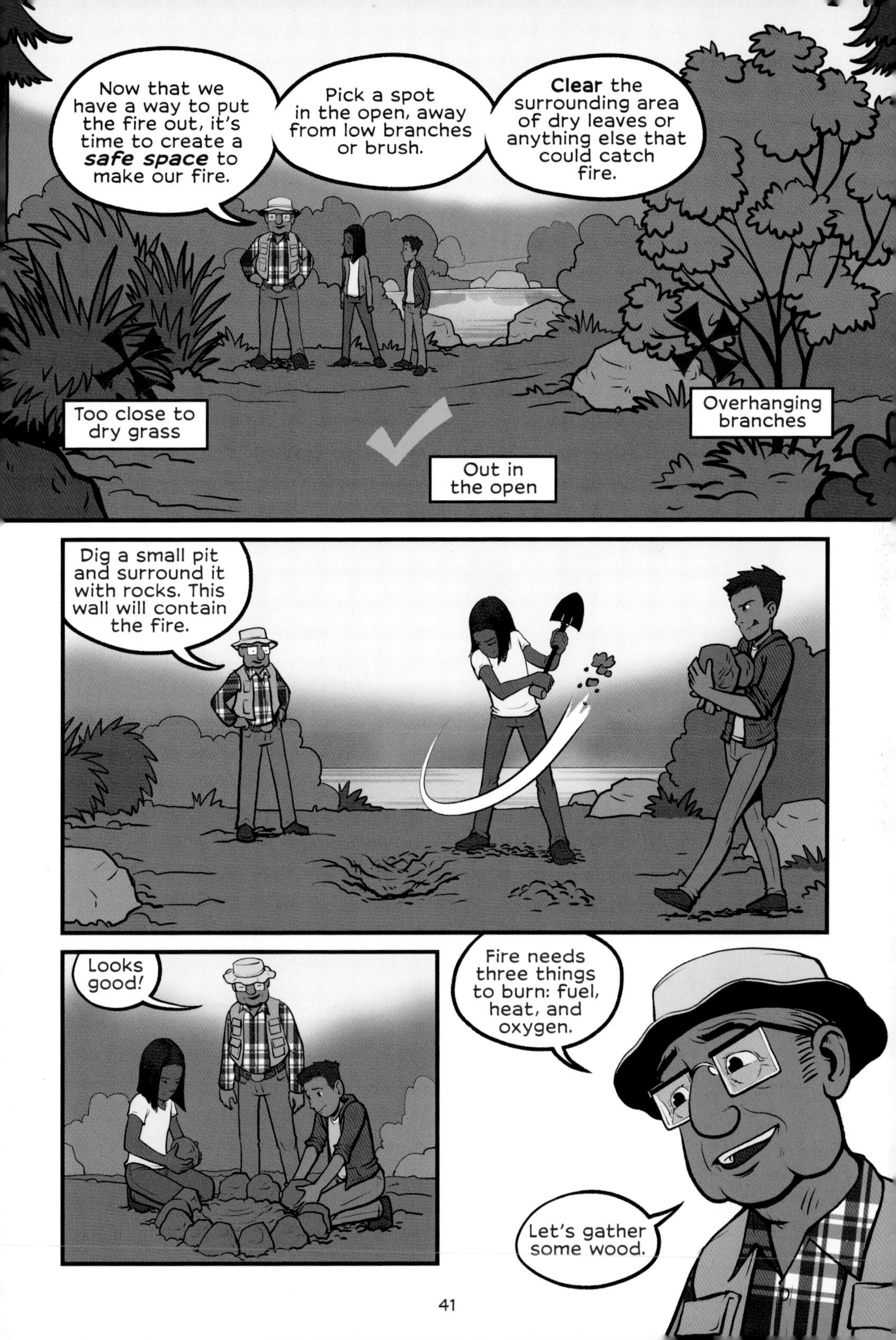

Now that we have a way to put the fire out, it’s time to create a ***safe space*** to make our fire.
Pick a spot in the open, away from low branches or brush.
**Clear** the surrounding area of dry leaves or anything else that could catch fire.
Too close to dry grass
Out in the open
Overhanging branches
Dig a small pit and surround it with rocks. This wall will contain the fire.
Looks good!
Fire needs three things to burn: fuel, heat, and oxygen.
Let’s gather some wood.

# Campfire Structure

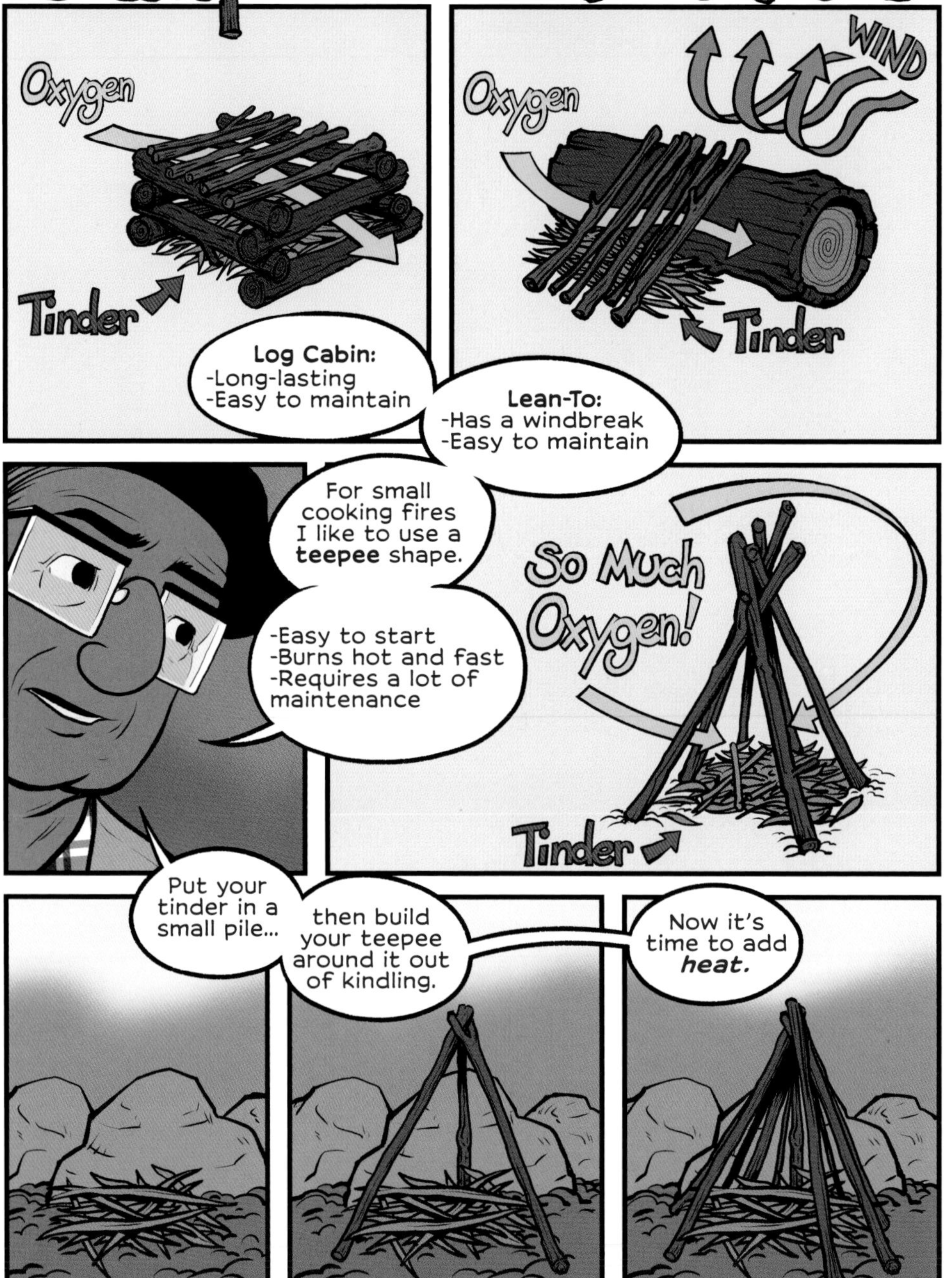
Oxygen
Tinder
Log Cabin:
-Long-lasting
-Easy to maintain
WIND
Oxygen
Tinder
Lean-To:
-Has a windbreak
-Easy to maintain
For small cooking fires I like to use a **teepee** shape.
-Easy to start
-Burns hot and fast
-Requires a lot of maintenance
So Much Oxygen!
Tinder
Put your tinder in a small pile...
then build your teepee around it out of kindling.
Now it's time to add ***heat.***

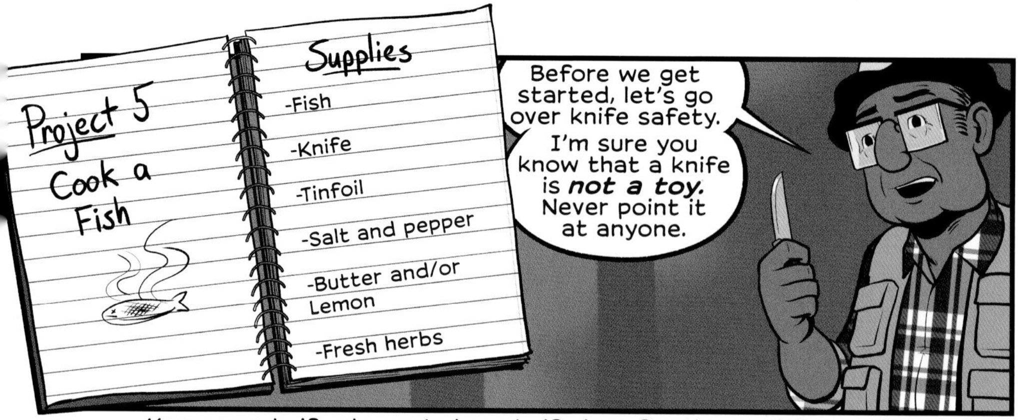
Project 5
Cook a Fish
Supplies
-Fish
-Knife
-Tinfoil
-Salt and pepper
-Butter and/or Lemon
-Fresh herbs
Before we get started, let's go over knife safety.
I'm sure you know that a knife is ***not a toy.*** Never point it at anyone.

Keep your knife sharp. A sharp knife is safer than a dull one since it is less likely to slip off the object you are cutting.

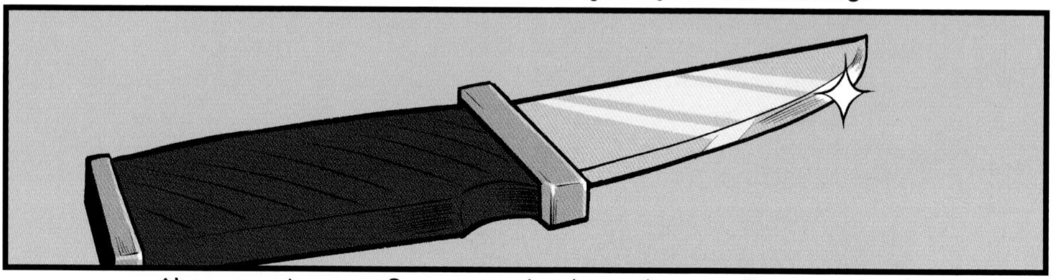

Always cut away from your body and away from anybody around you. Think about where the knife will go if it slips.

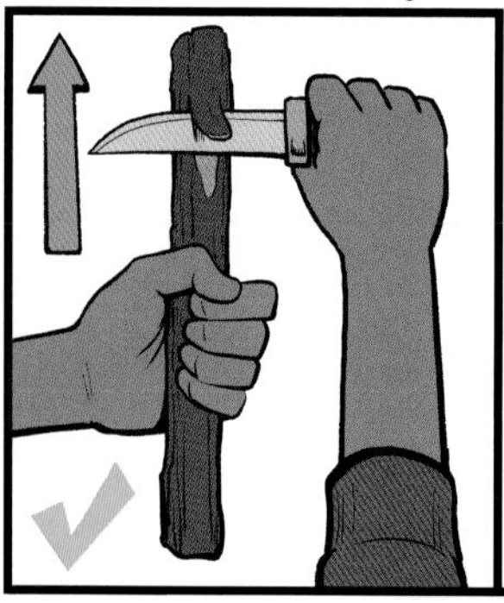

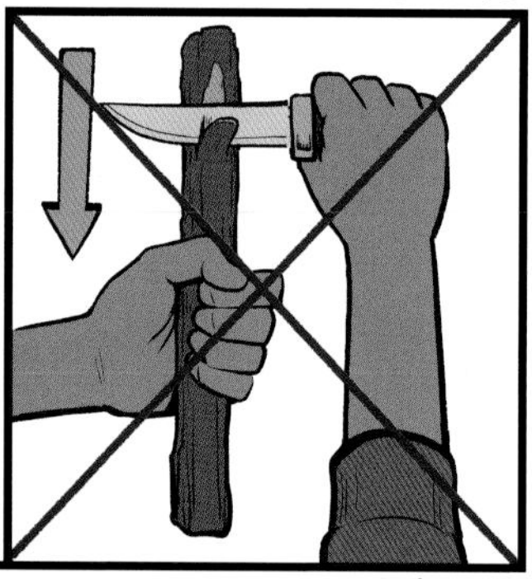

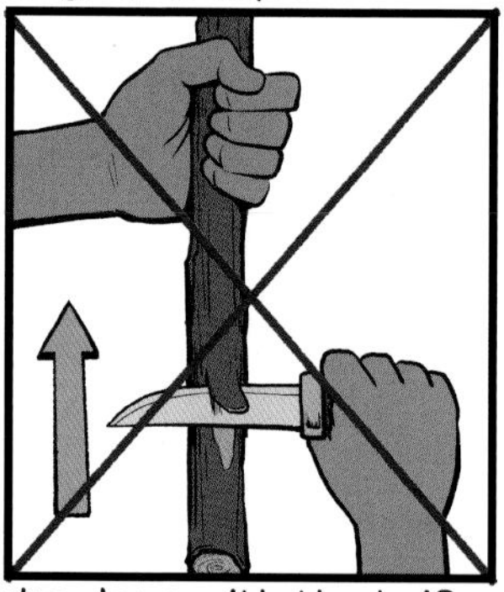

Carving away from your body with your elbows on your knees is a really safe position. It protects the femoral arteries on your inner thighs.

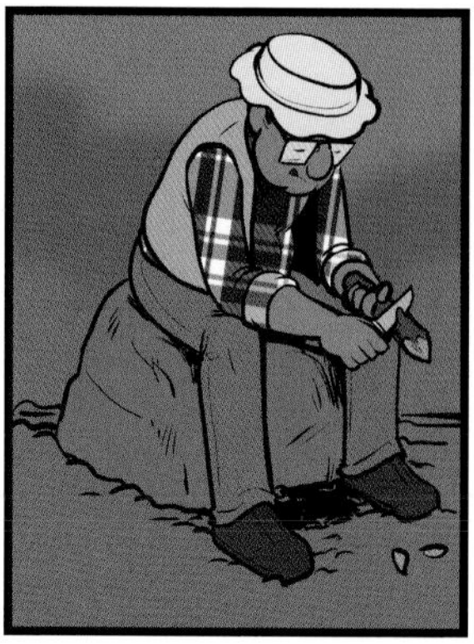

When you're done with the knife, put it back in its sheath or fold it.

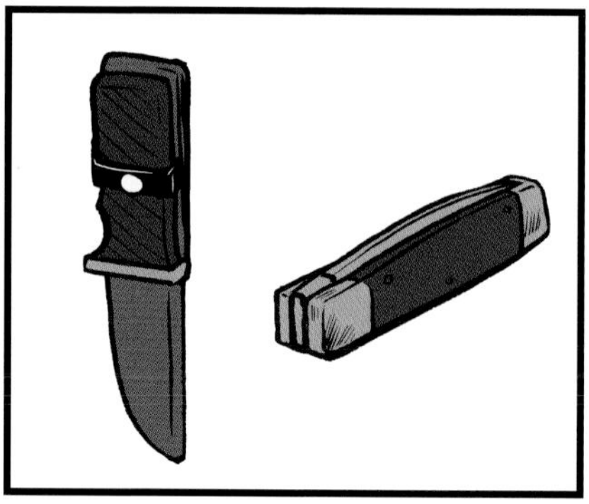

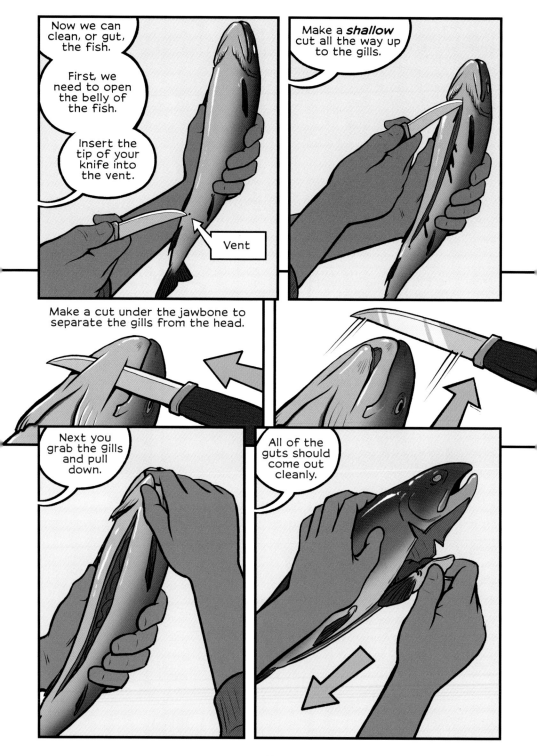

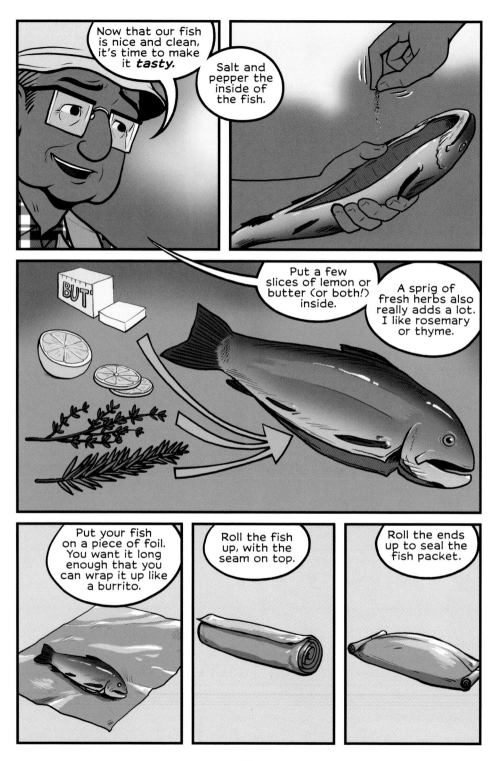

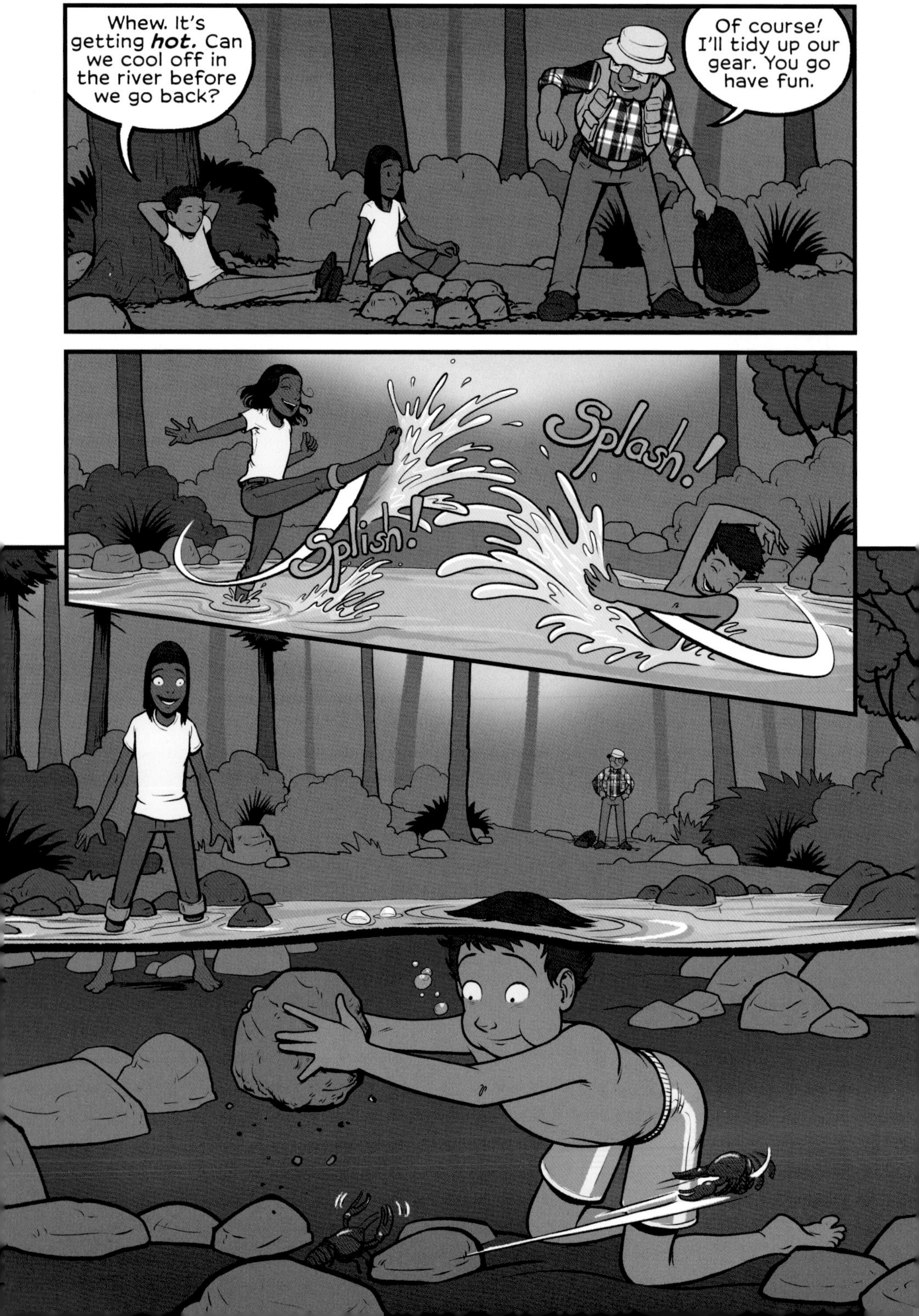
Whew. It's getting *hot.* Can we cool off in the river before we go back?
Of course! I'll tidy up our gear. You go have fun.
Splash!
Splish!

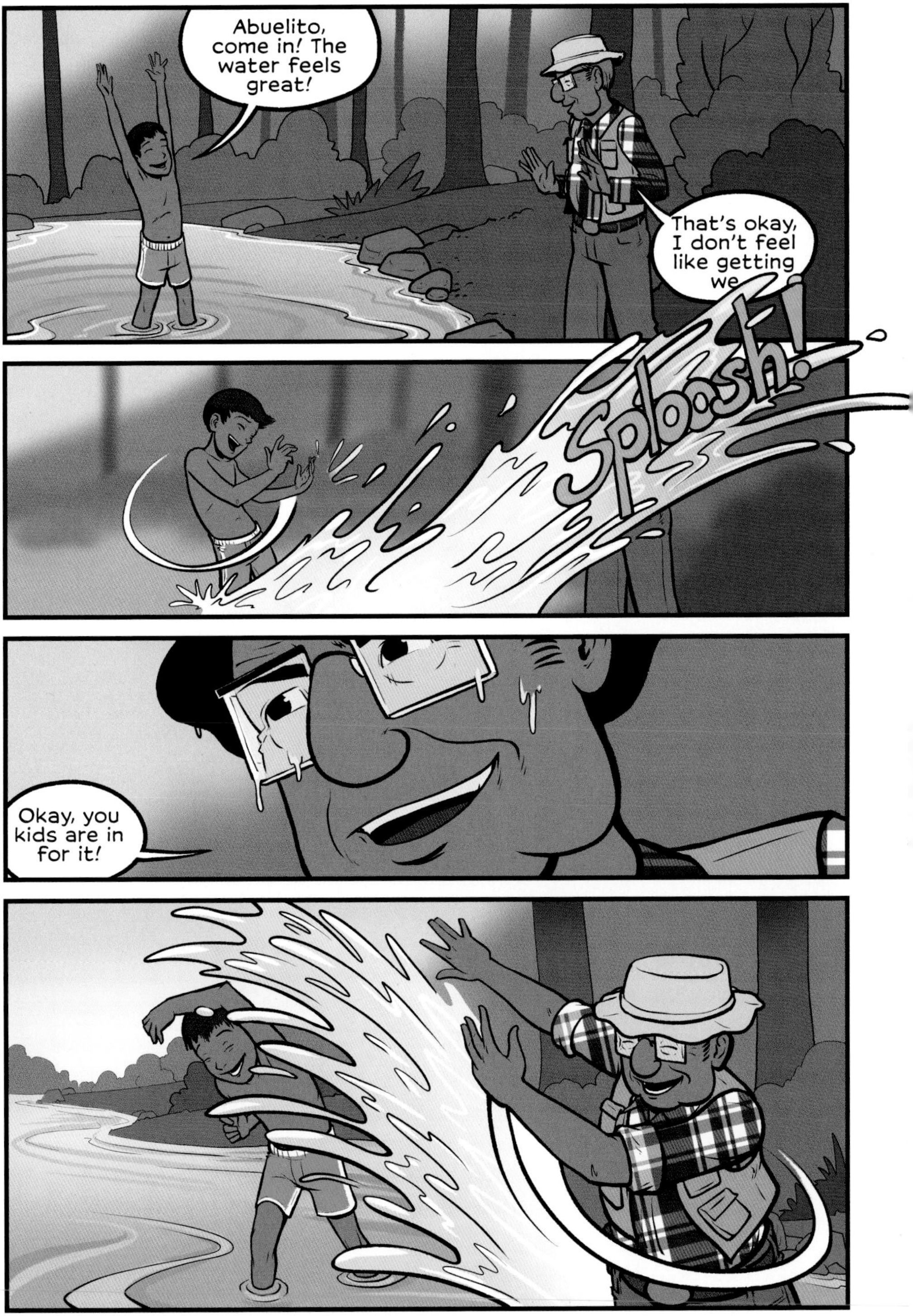
Abuelito, come in! The water feels great!
That's okay, I don't feel like getting we
Sploosh!
Okay, you kids are in for it!

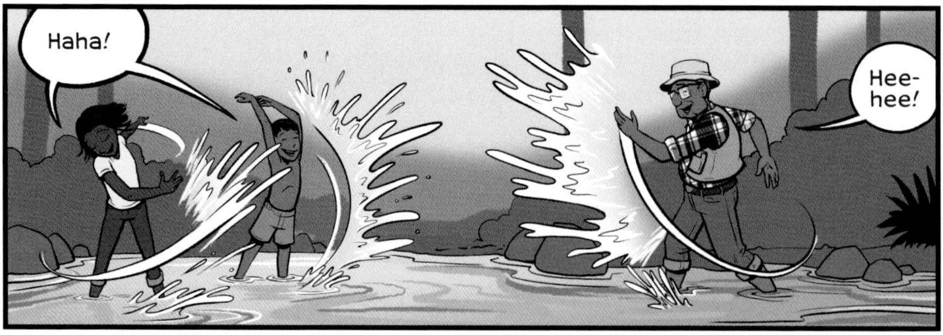
Haha!
Hee-
hee!

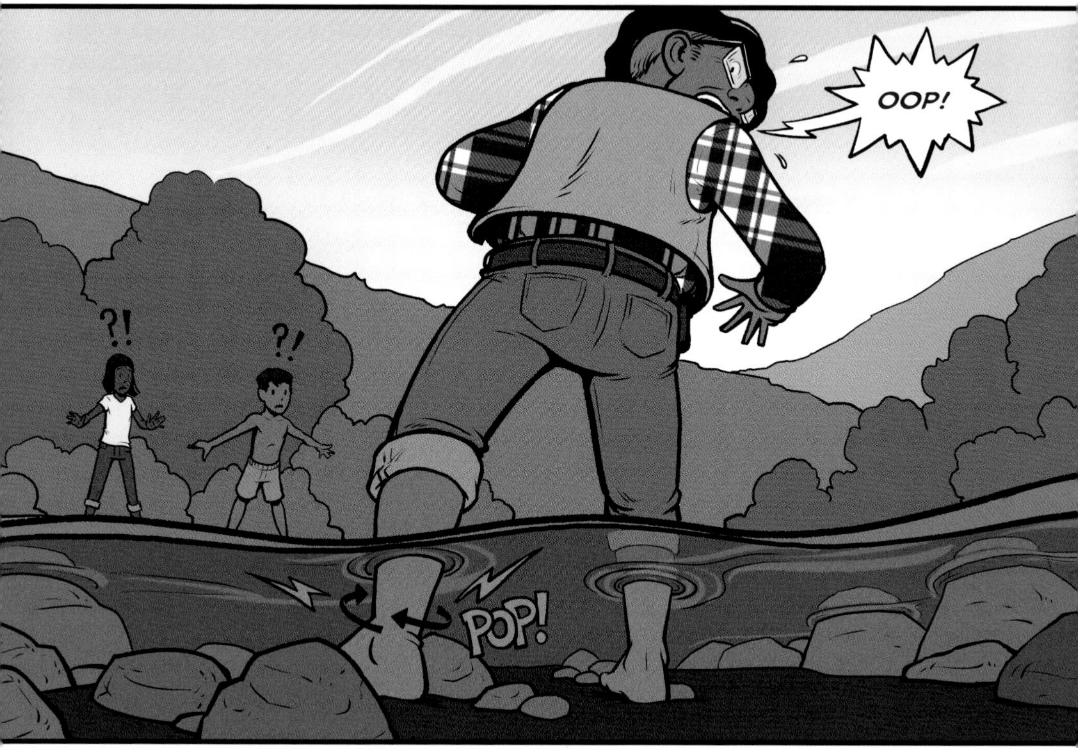
OOP!
?!
?!
POP!

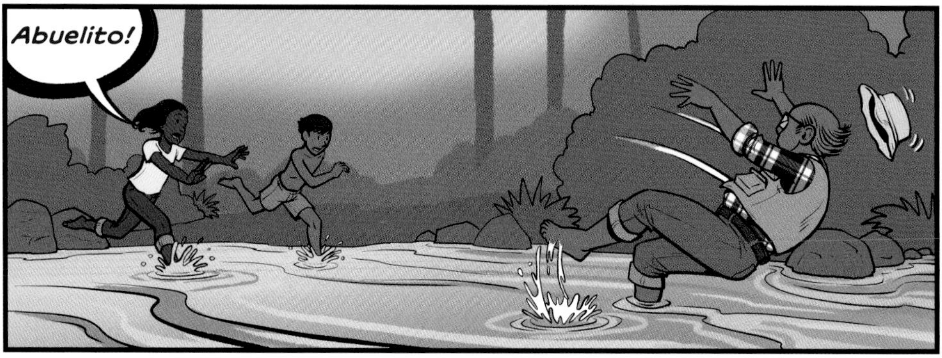
Abuelito!

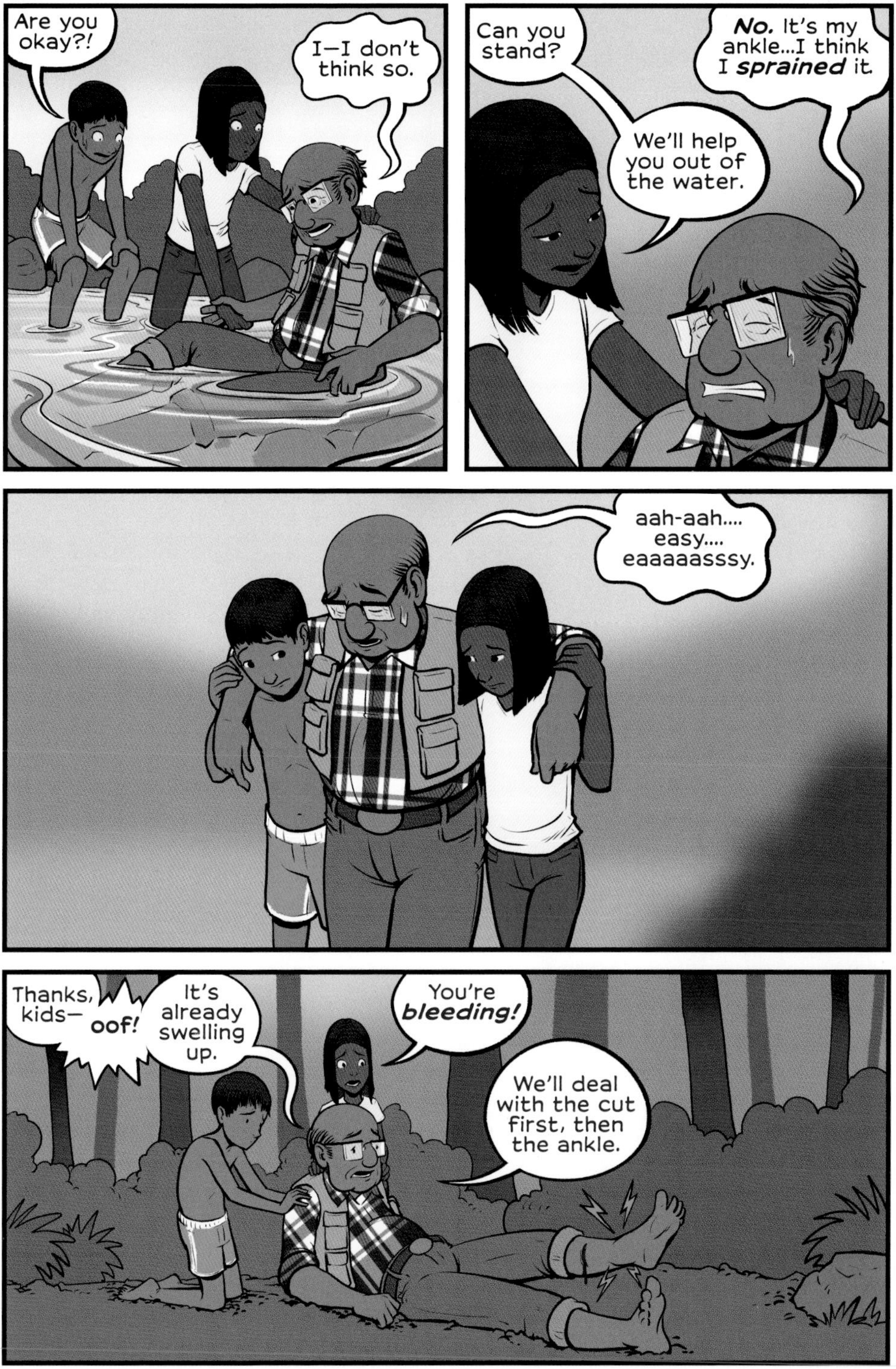

Are you okay?!
I—I don't think so.
Can you stand?
**No.** It's my ankle...I think I ***sprained*** it.
We'll help you out of the water.
aah-aah.... easy.... eaaaaasssy.
Thanks, kids— **oof!**
It's already swelling up.
You're ***bleeding!***
We'll deal with the cut first, then the ankle.

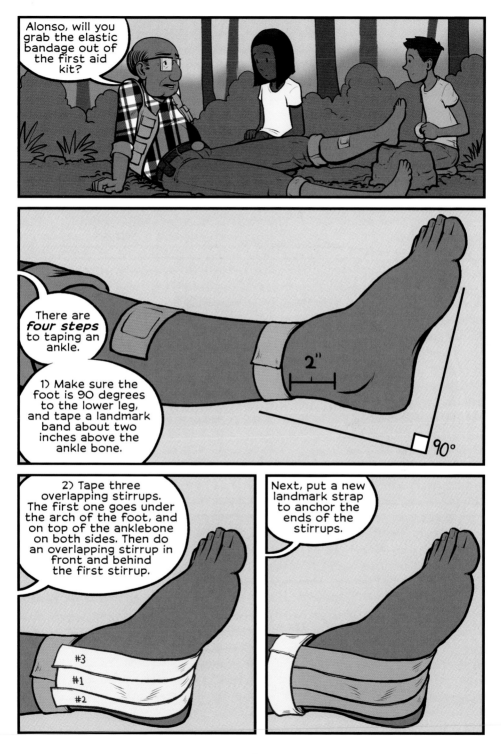

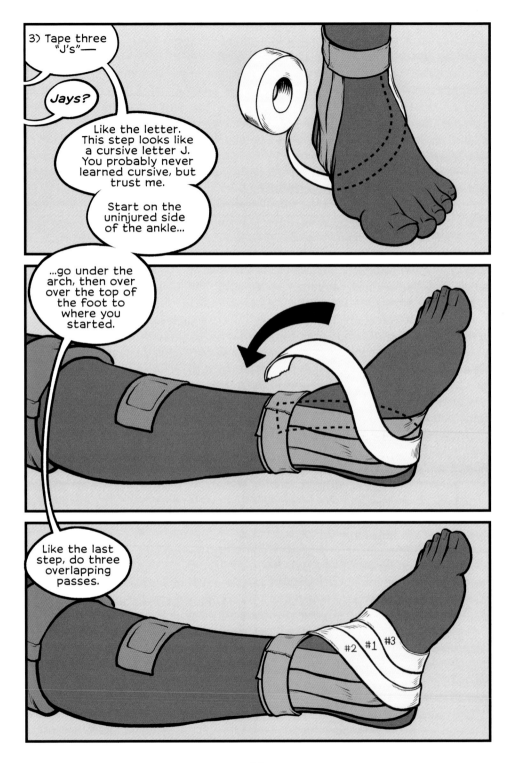

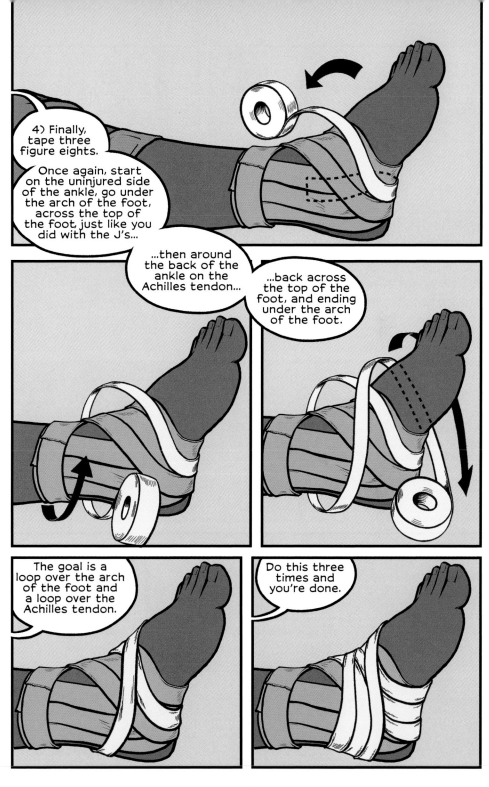

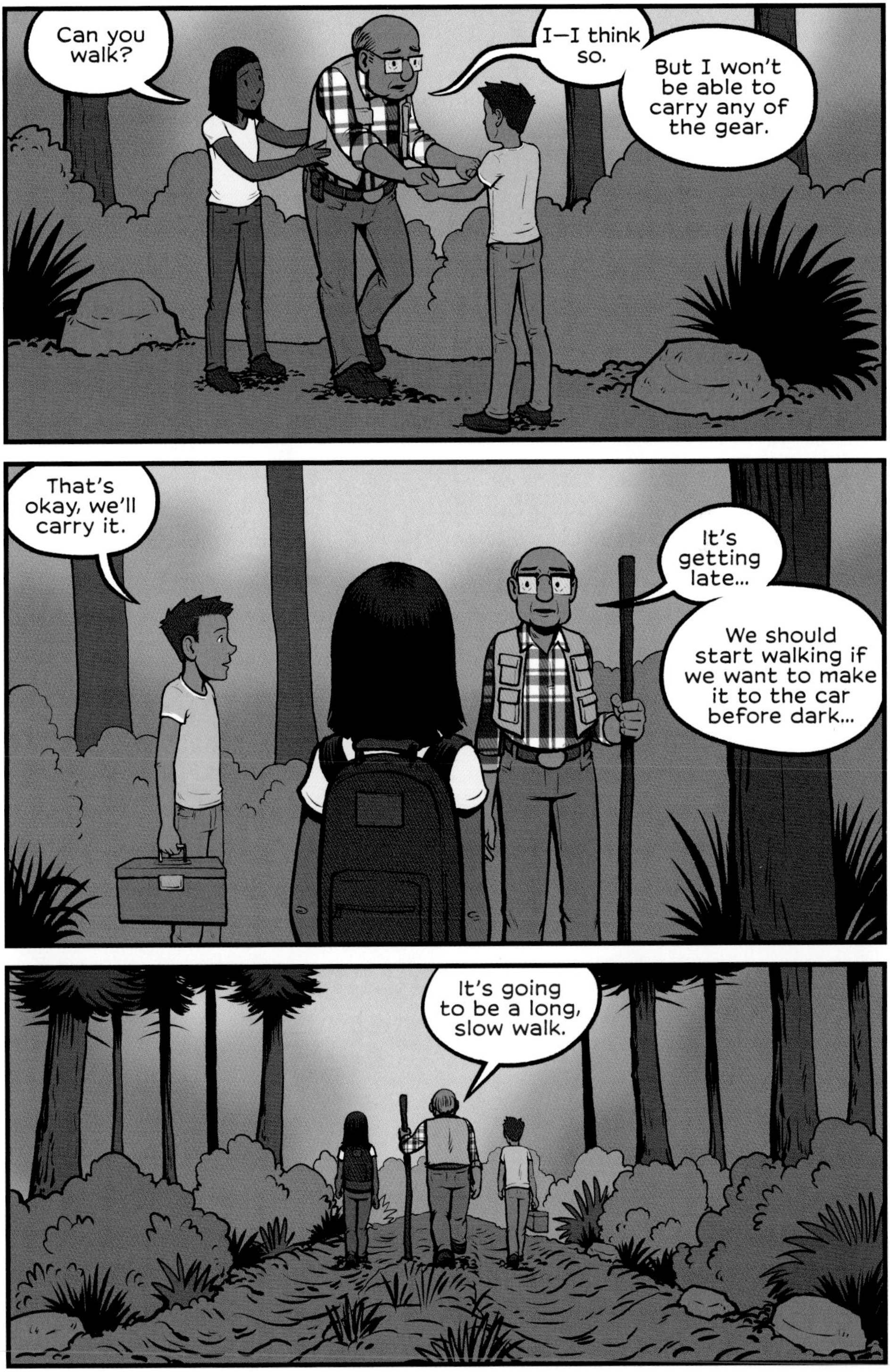
Can you walk?
I—I think so.
But I won't be able to carry any of the gear.
That's okay, we'll carry it.
It's getting late...
We should start walking if we want to make it to the car before dark...
It's going to be a long, slow walk.

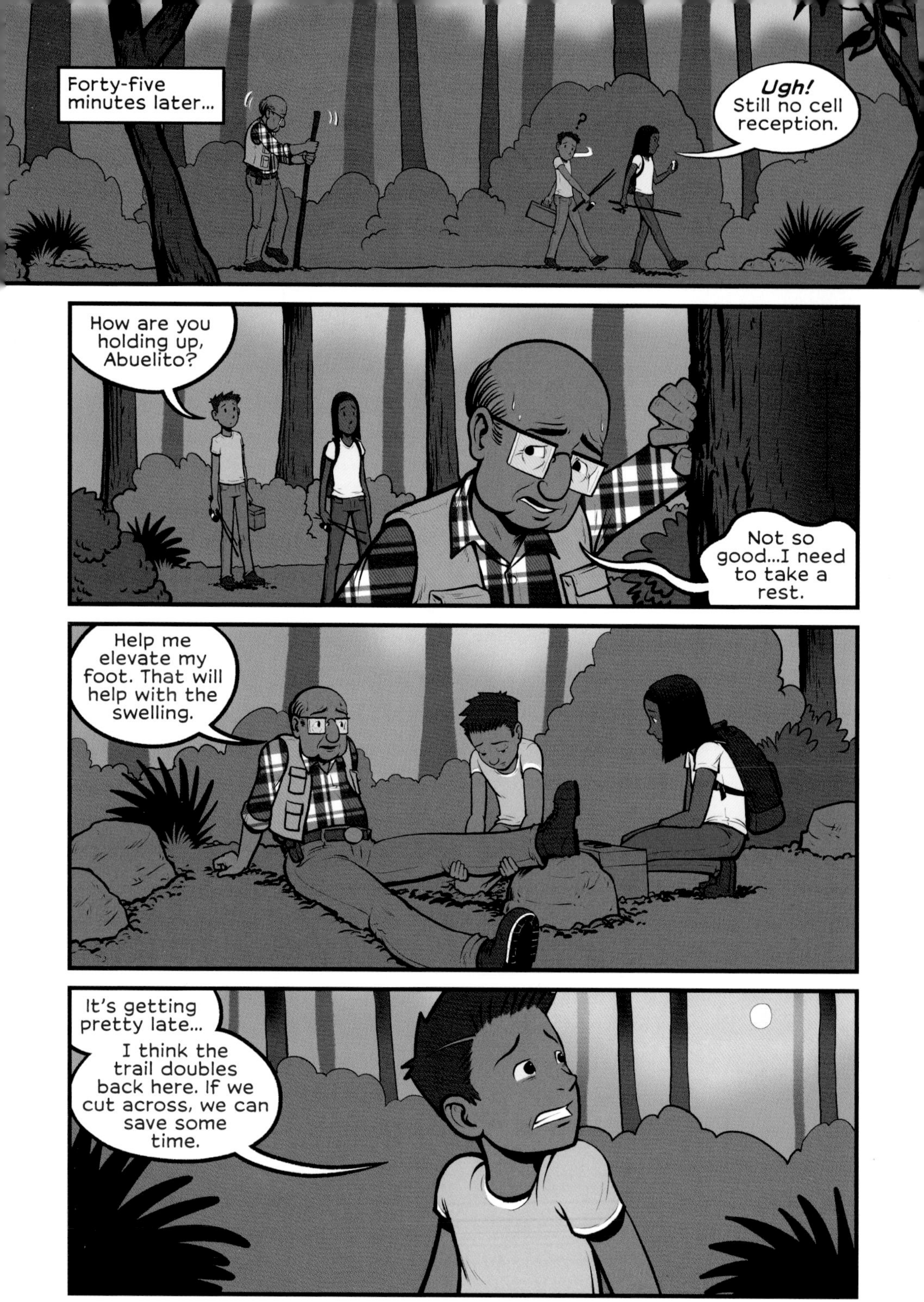
Forty-five minutes later...
*Ugh!* Still no cell reception.
How are you holding up, Abuelito?
Not so good...I need to take a rest.
Help me elevate my foot. That will help with the swelling.
It's getting pretty late...
I think the trail doubles back here. If we cut across, we can save some time.

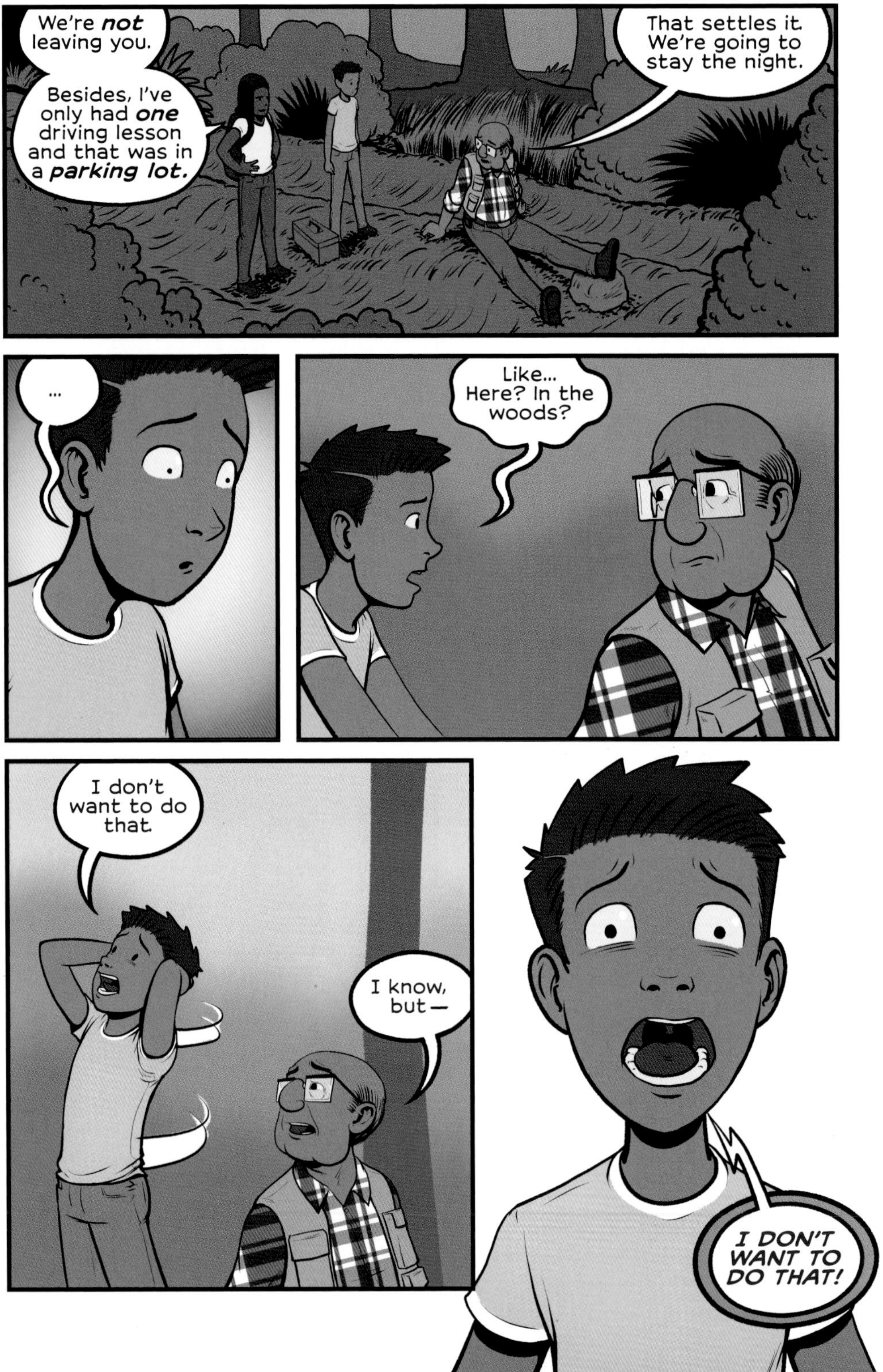
We're *not* leaving you.
Besides, I've only had *one* driving lesson and that was in a *parking lot.*
That settles it. We're going to stay the night.
...
Like... Here? In the woods?
I don't want to do that.
I know, but—
*I DON'T WANT TO DO THAT!*

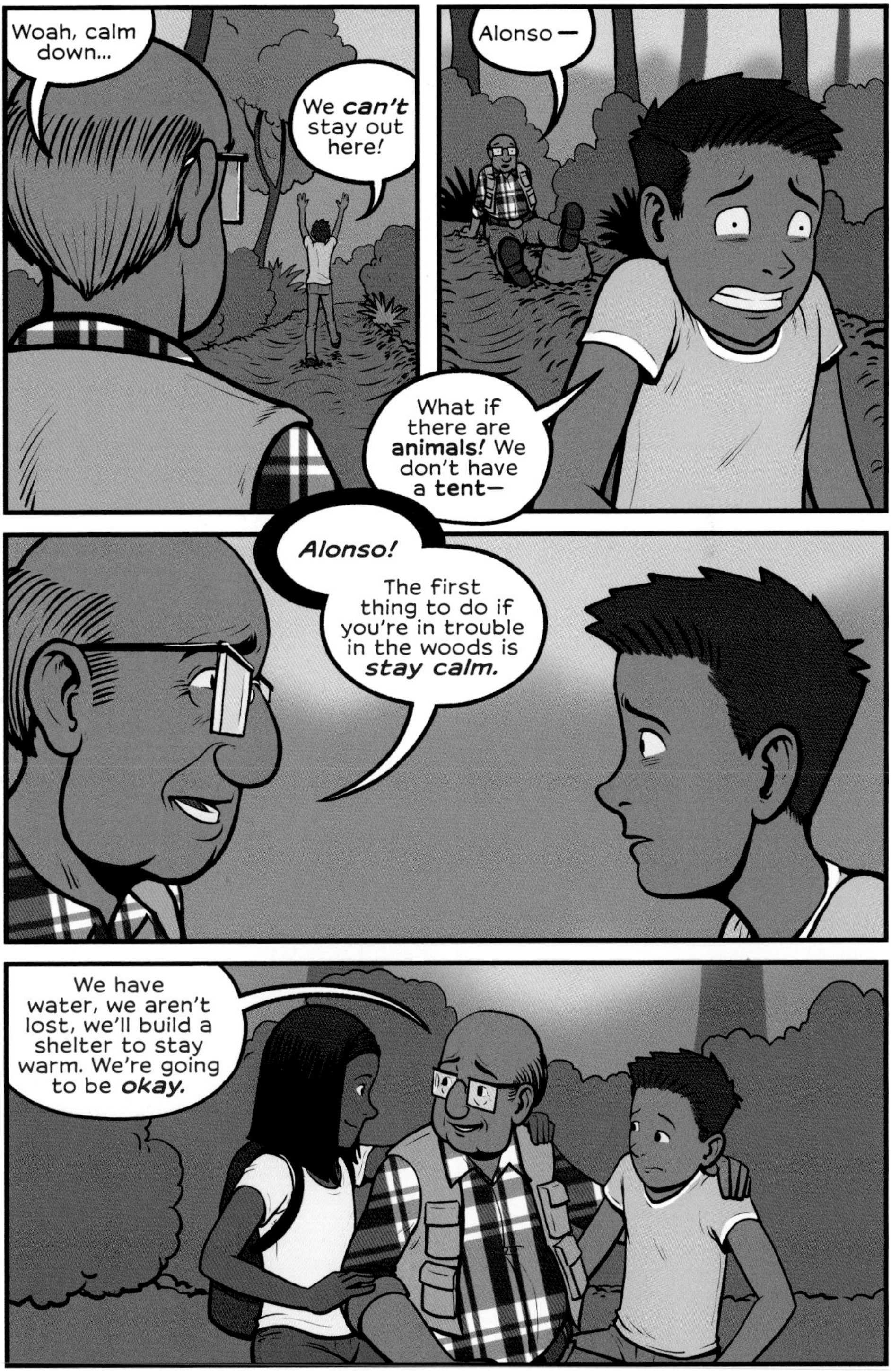
Woah, calm down...
We *can't* stay out here!
Alonso—
What if there are **animals!** We don't have a **tent—**
***Alonso!***
The first thing to do if you're in trouble in the woods is ***stay calm.***
We have water, we aren't lost, we'll build a shelter to stay warm. We're going to be ***okay.***

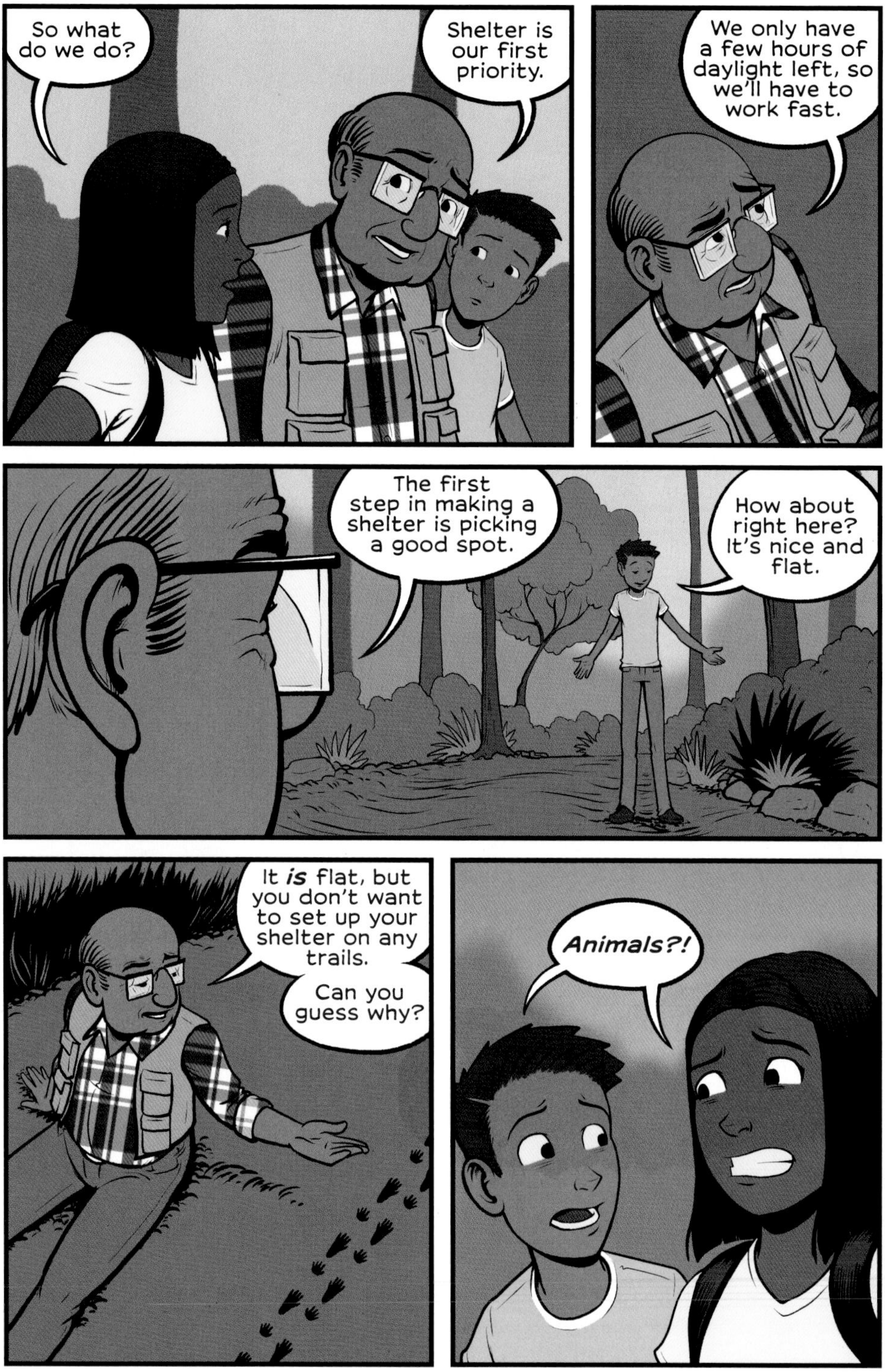

So what do we do?
Shelter is our first priority.
We only have a few hours of daylight left, so we'll have to work fast.
The first step in making a shelter is picking a good spot.
How about right here? It's nice and flat.
It *is* flat, but you don't want to set up your shelter on any trails.
Can you guess why?
Animals?!

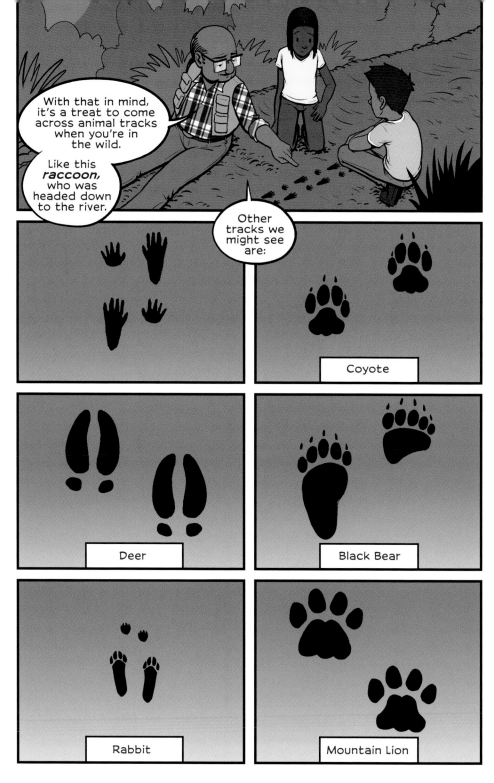

Okay, we're off the trail. Anything else we should look out for?
When choosing a site for a shelter, we want to consider the **Five W's:** Widowmakers Wind Water Wood Wildlife
*Widowmakers:* Look out for dead branches dangling from trees that can fall on you.
*Wind:* You want to be away from the wind or set your shelter up to block the wind.
*Water:* Close to water for drinking and putting out the fire but also to make sure water runs through camp if it rains.
*Wood:* Enough to build a shelter and for an all-night campfire.
*Wildlife:* Don't camp on trails and look out for insect and animal dens like holes and rotting logs.

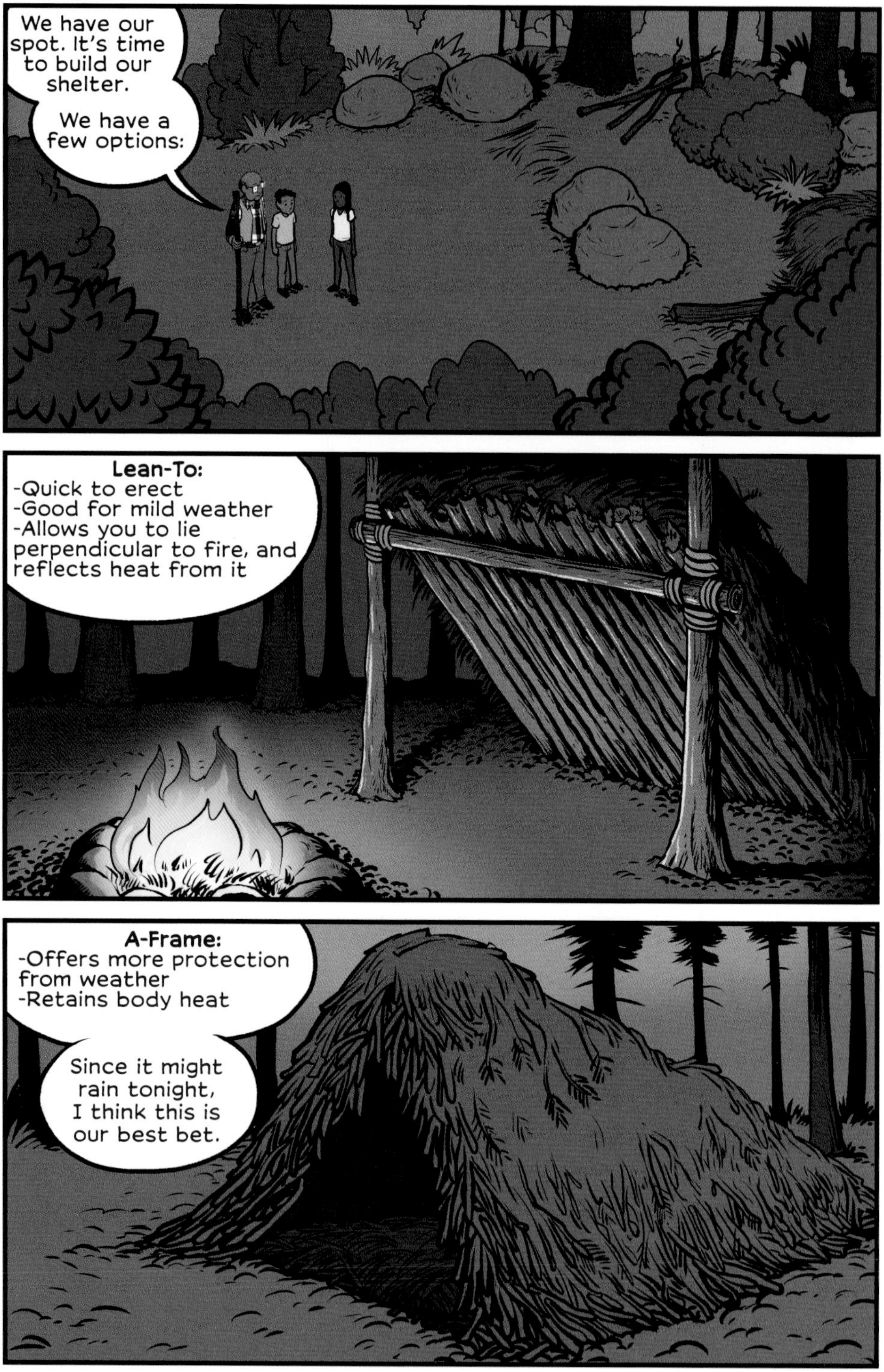
We have our spot. It's time to build our shelter.
We have a few options:
Lean-To:
-Quick to erect
-Good for mild weather
-Allows you to lie perpendicular to fire, and reflects heat from it
A-Frame:
-Offers more protection from weather
-Retains body heat
Since it might rain tonight, I think this is our best bet.

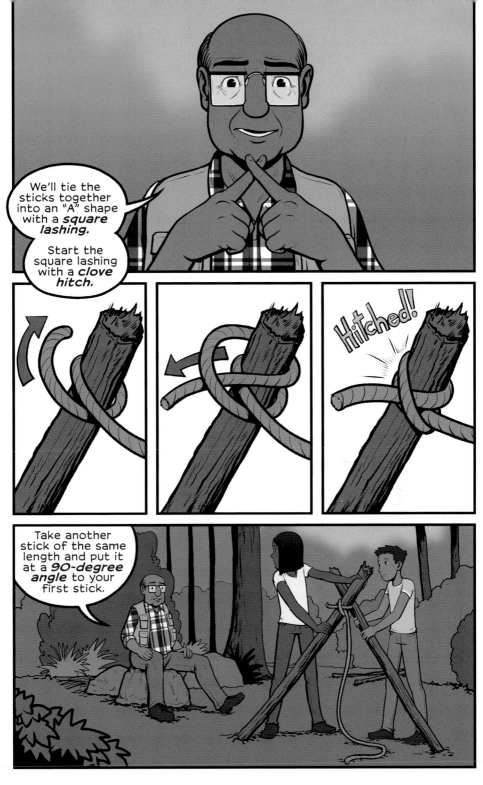

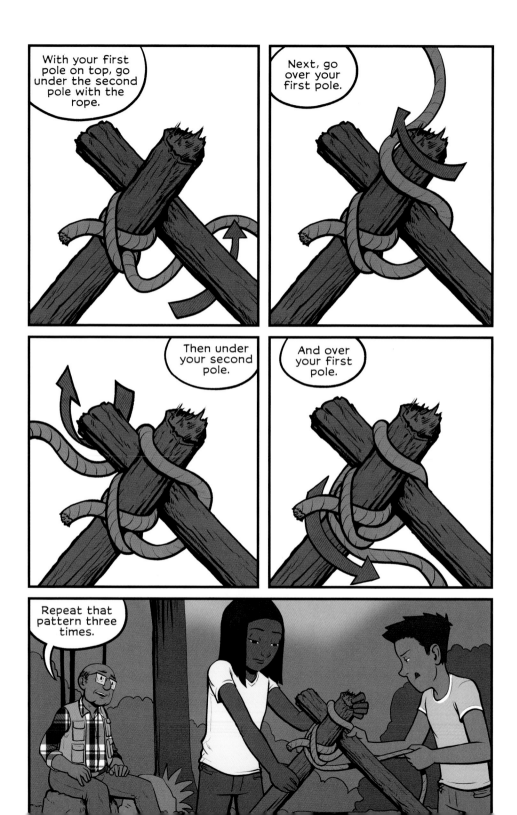

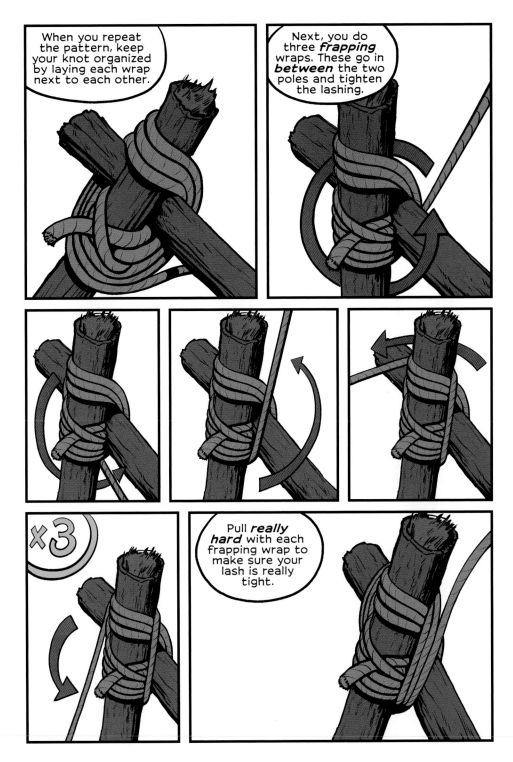

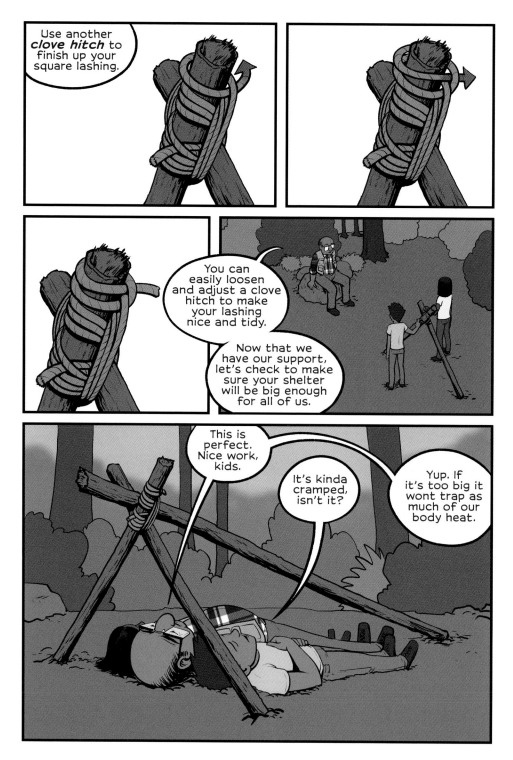

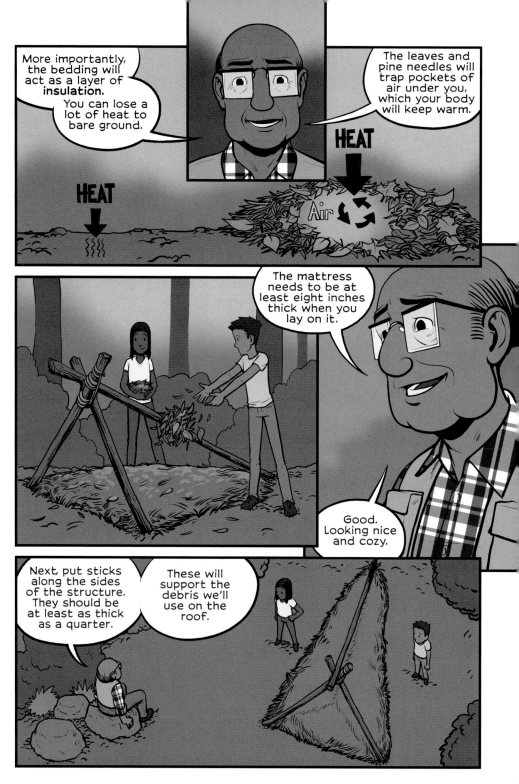

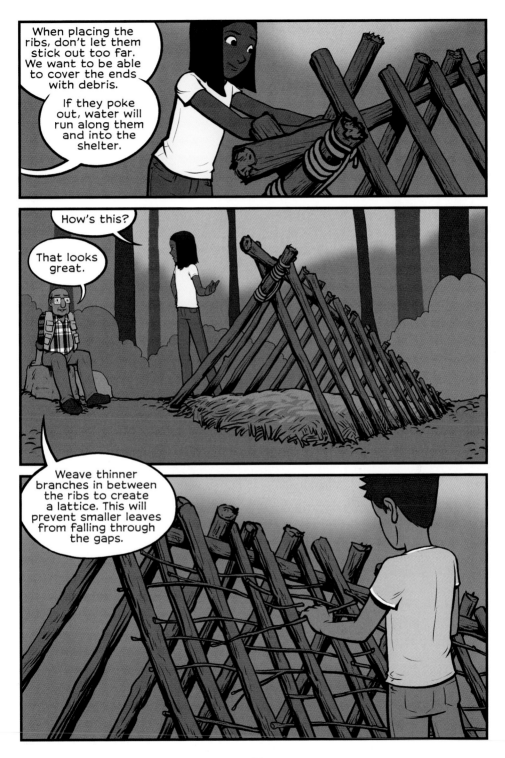

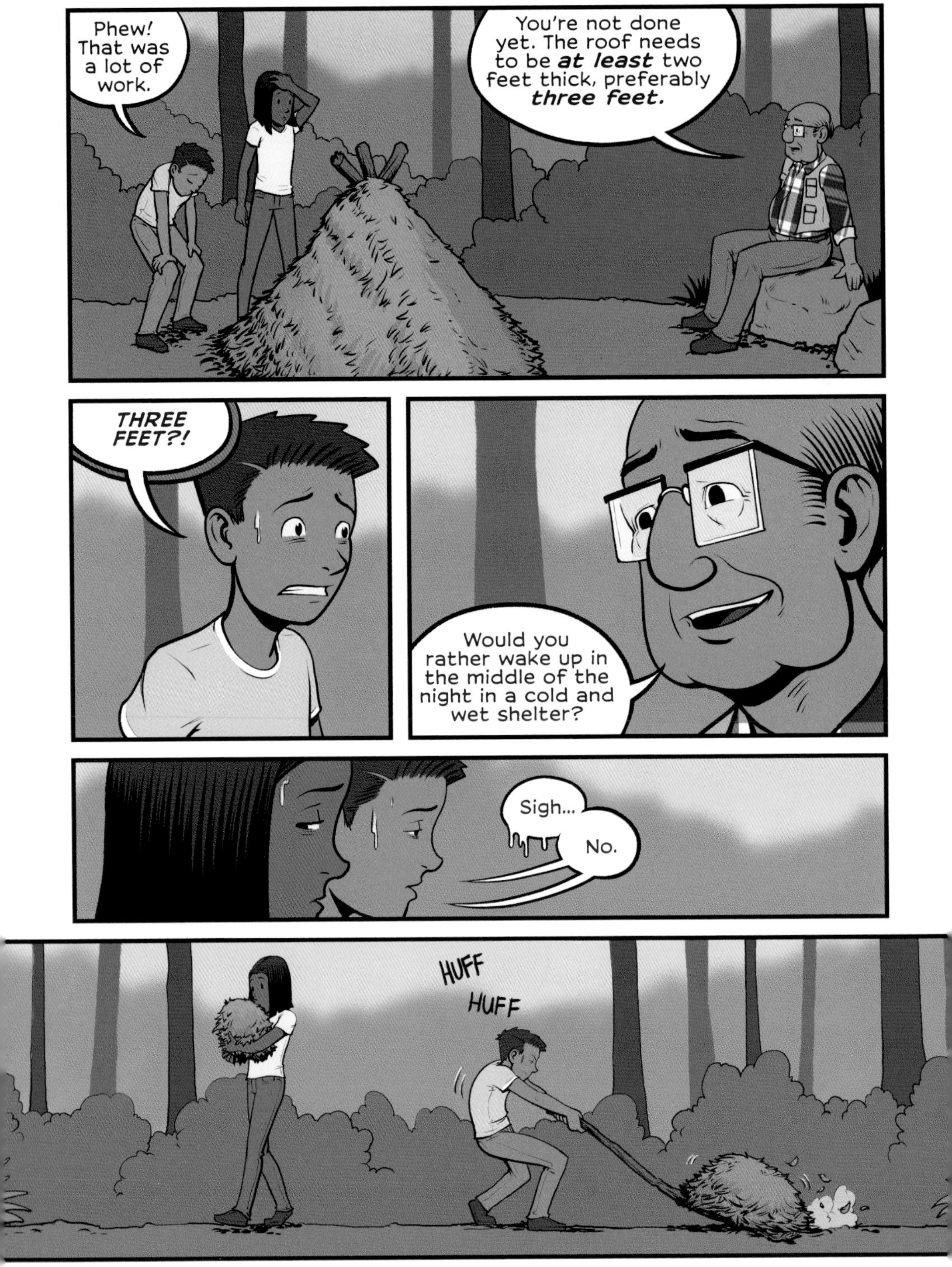
Phew! That was a lot of work.
You're not done yet. The roof needs to be **at least** two feet thick, preferably ***three feet.***
***THREE FEET?!***
Would you rather wake up in the middle of the night in a cold and wet shelter?
Sigh...
No.
HUFF
HUFF

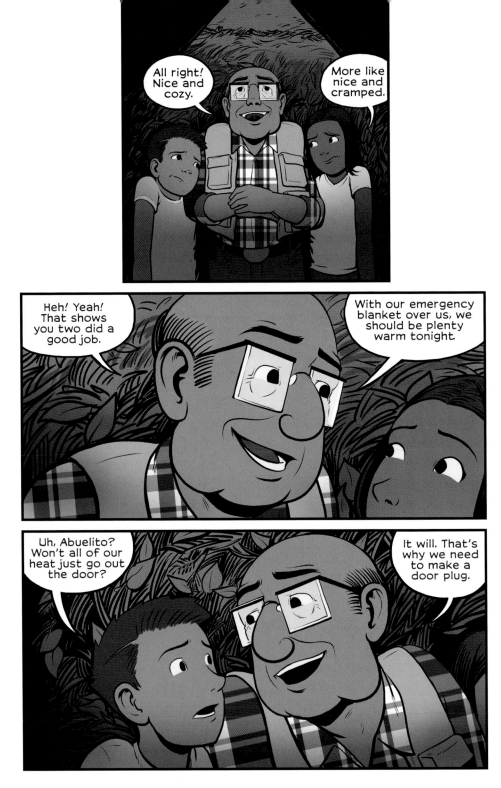

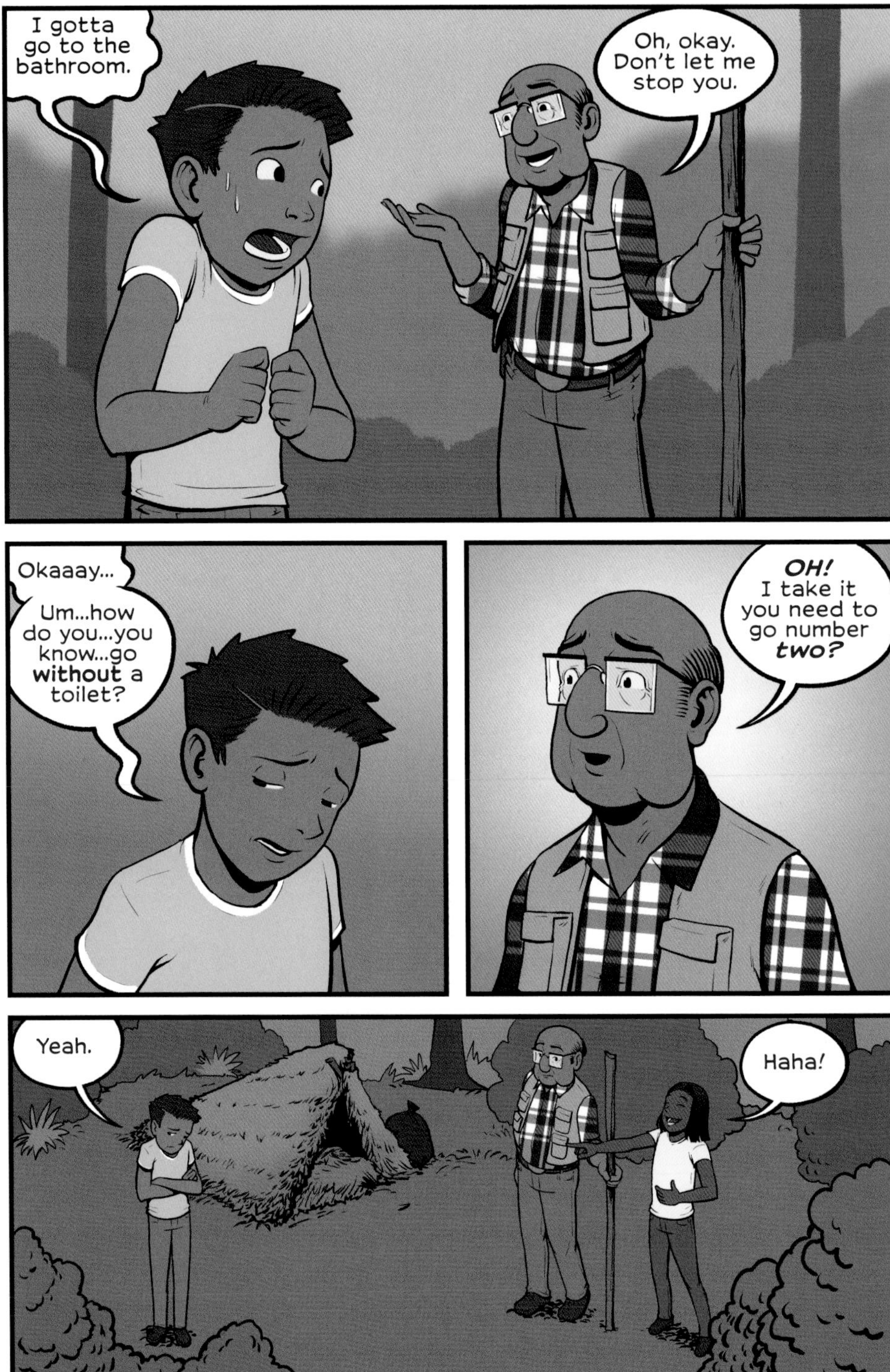
I gotta go to the bathroom.
Oh, okay. Don't let me stop you.
Okaaay...
Um...how do you...you know...go **without** a toilet?
***OH!*** I take it you need to go number ***two?***
Yeah.
Haha!

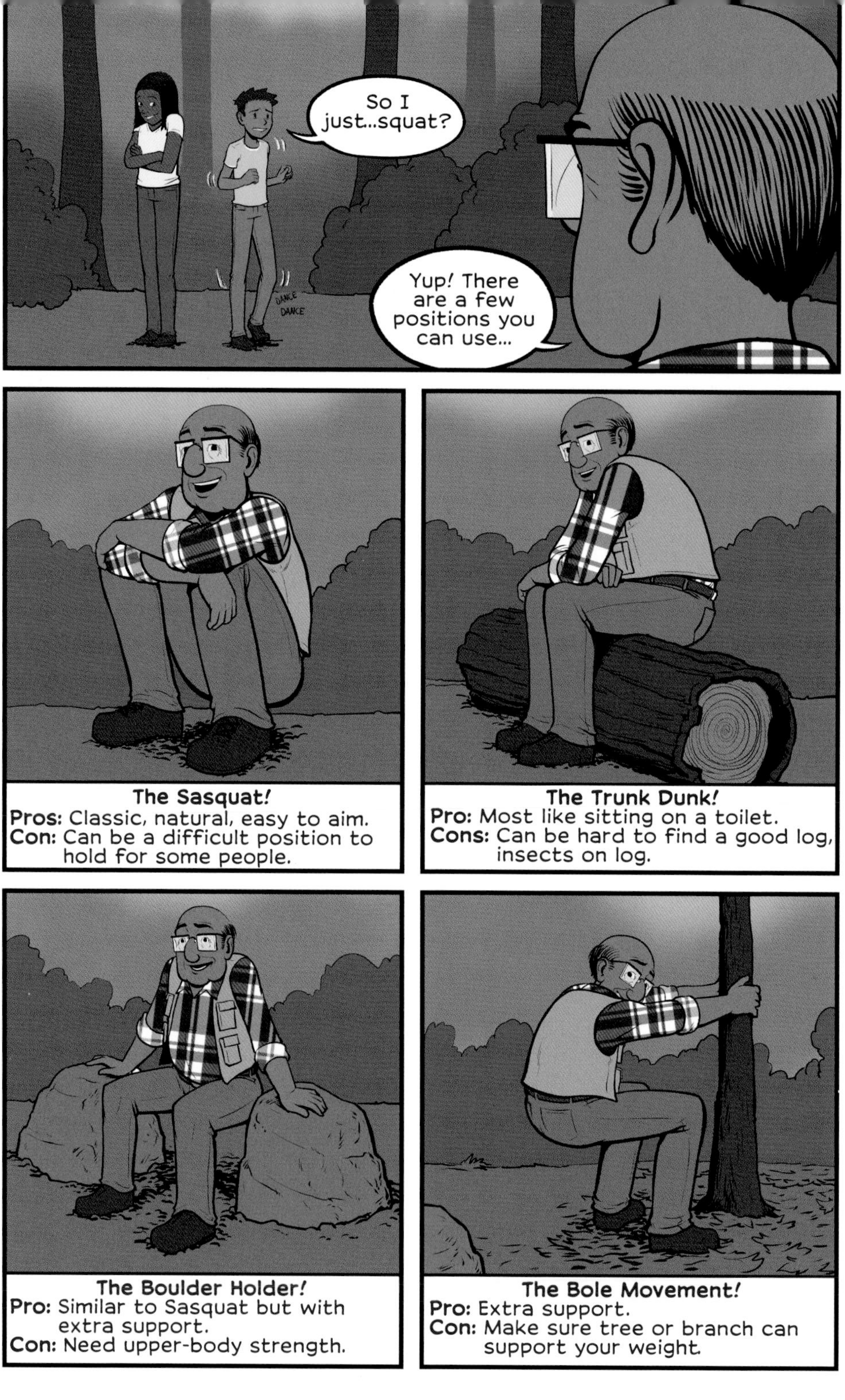
So I just...squat?
DANCE
DANCE
Yup! There are a few positions you can use...
The Sasquat!
Pros: Classic, natural, easy to aim.
Con: Can be a difficult position to hold for some people.
The Trunk Dunk!
Pro: Most like sitting on a toilet.
Cons: Can be hard to find a good log, insects on log.
The Boulder Holder!
Pro: Similar to Sasquat but with extra support.
Con: Need upper-body strength.
The Bole Movement!
Pro: Extra support.
Con: Make sure tree or branch can support your weight.

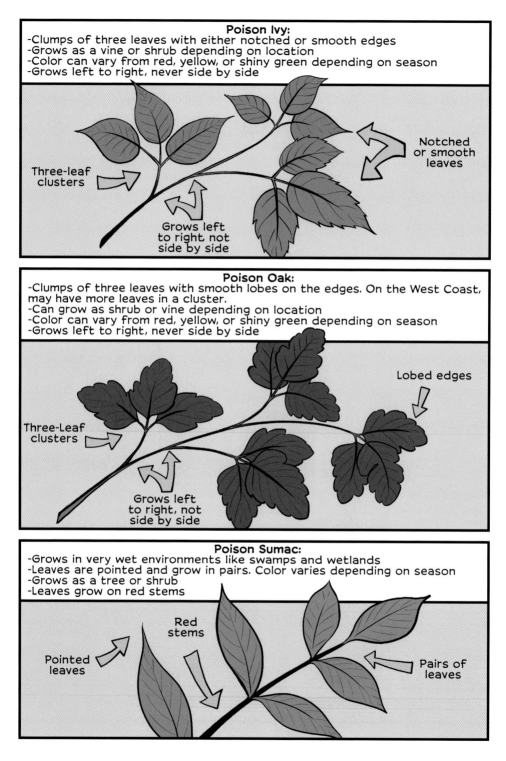

**Poison Ivy:**

- -Clumps of three leaves with either notched or smooth edges
- -Grows as a vine or shrub depending on location
- -Color can vary from red, yellow, or shiny green depending on season
- -Grows left to right, never side by side

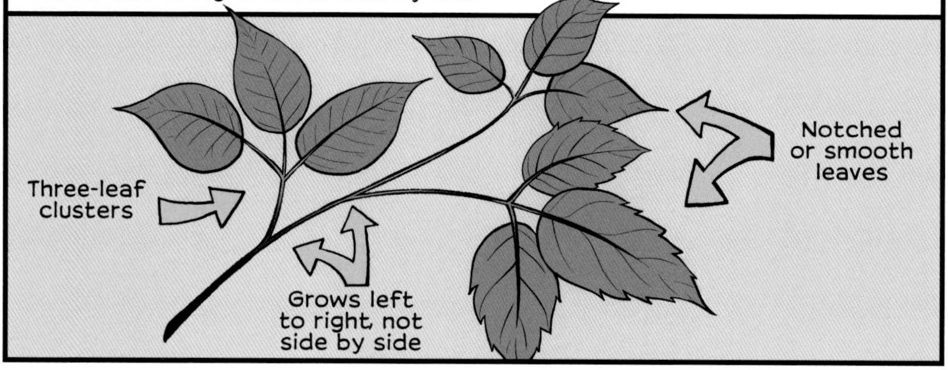
Three-leaf clusters
Grows left to right, not side by side
Notched or smooth leaves

**Poison Oak:**

- -Clumps of three leaves with smooth lobes on the edges. On the West Coast, may have more leaves in a cluster.
- -Can grow as shrub or vine depending on location
- -Color can vary from red, yellow, or shiny green depending on season
- -Grows left to right, never side by side

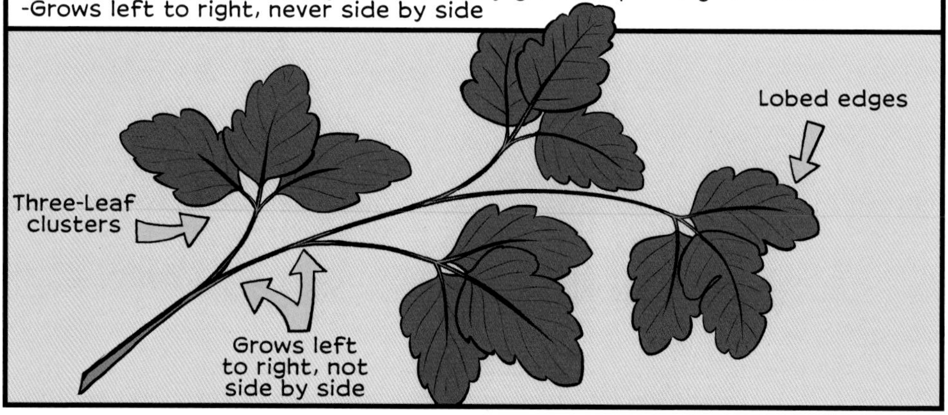
Three-Leaf clusters
Grows left to right, not side by side
Lobed edges

**Poison Sumac:**

- -Grows in very wet environments like swamps and wetlands
- -Leaves are pointed and grow in pairs. Color varies depending on season
- -Grows as a tree or shrub
- -Leaves grow on red stems

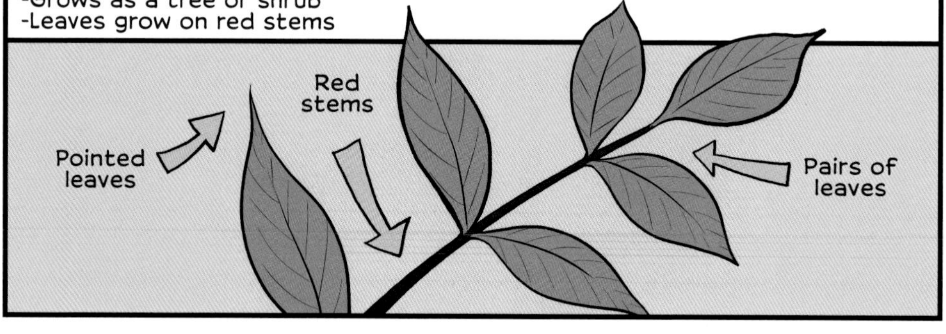
Pointed leaves
Red stems
Pairs of leaves

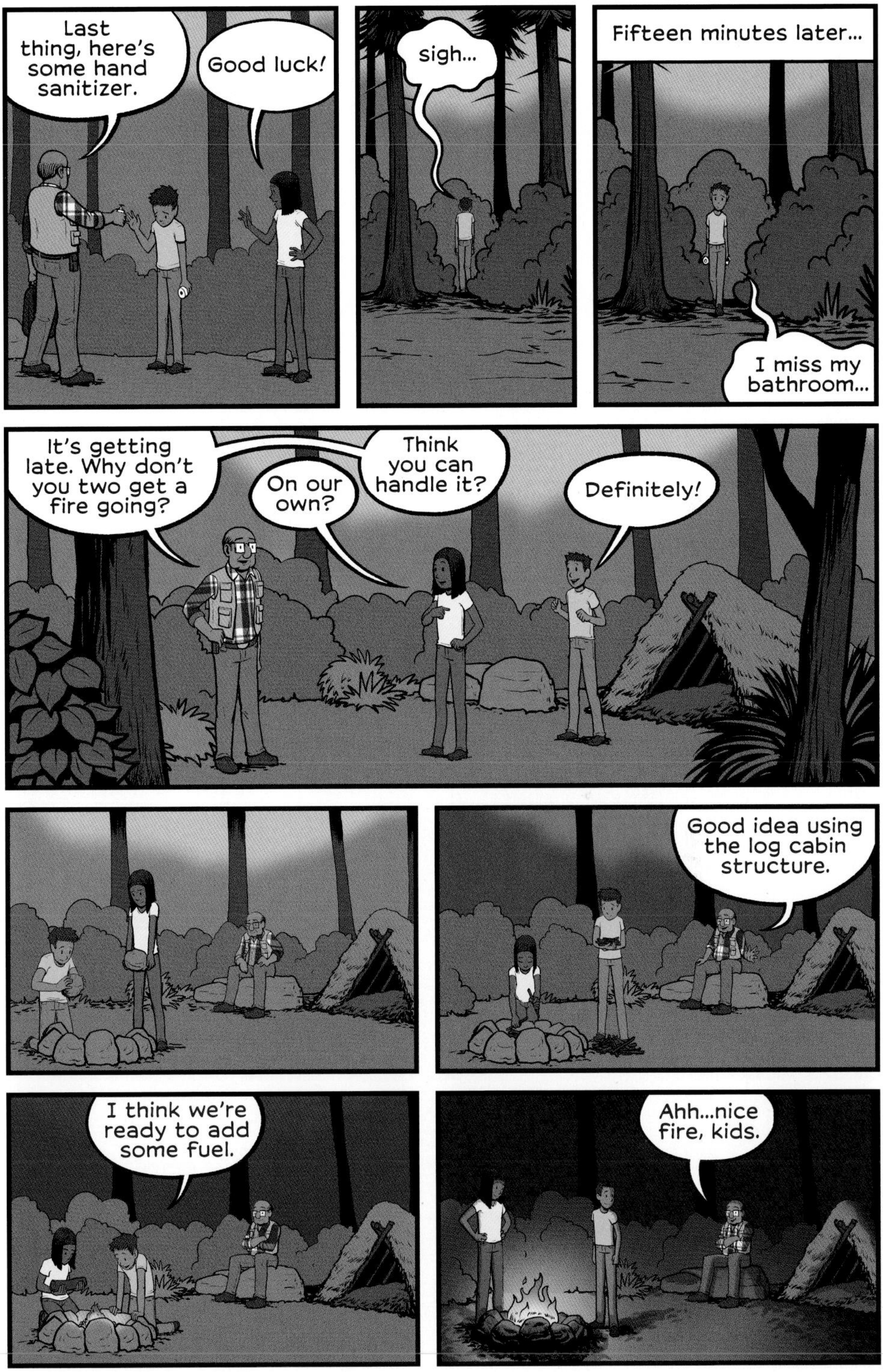
Last thing, here's some hand sanitizer.
Good luck!
sigh...
Fifteen minutes later...
I miss my bathroom...
It's getting late. Why don't you two get a fire going?
On our own?
Think you can handle it?
Definitely!
Good idea using the log cabin structure.
I think we're ready to add some fuel.
Ahh...nice fire, kids.

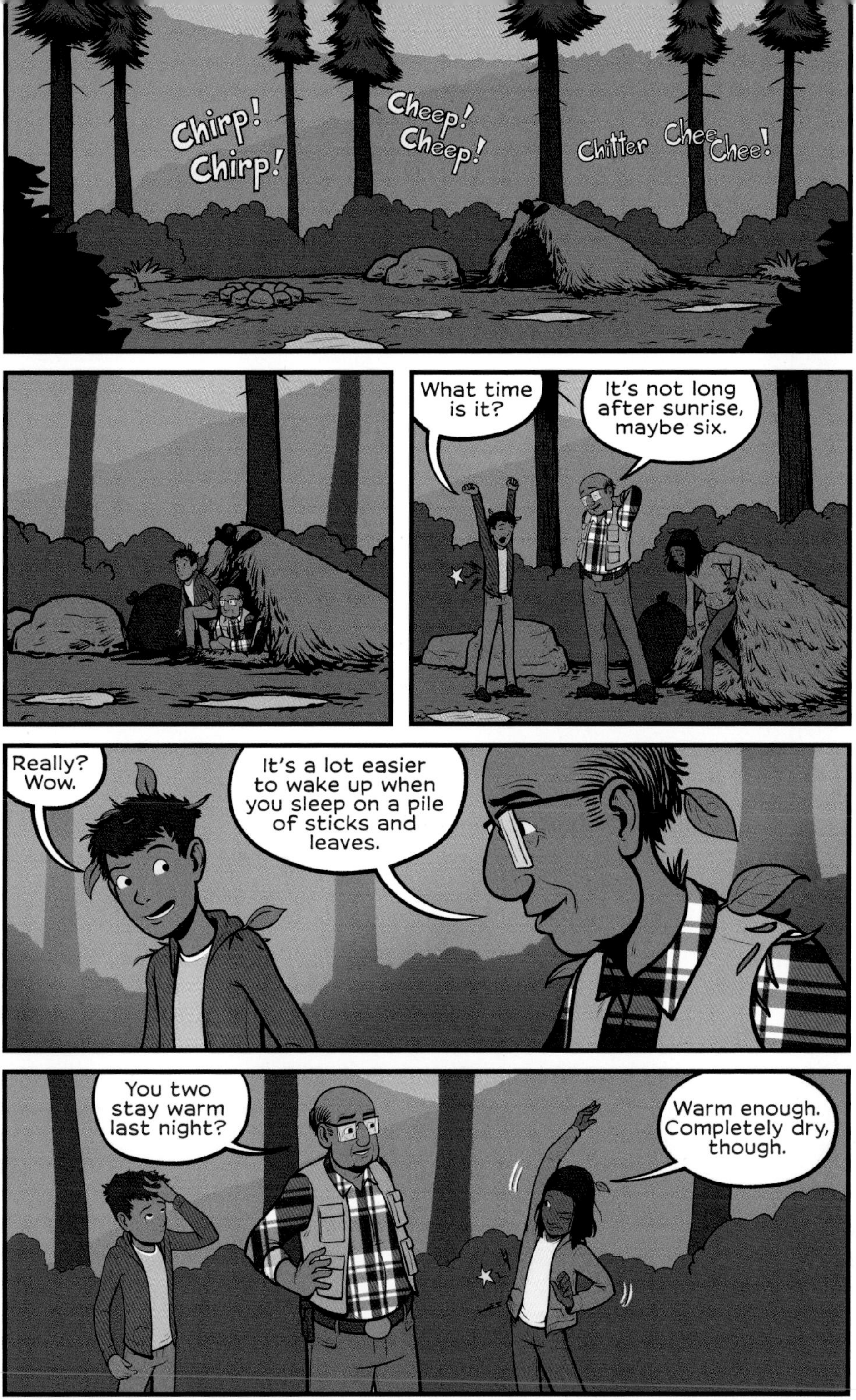
Chirp! Chirp!
Cheep! Cheep!
Chitter Chee Chee!
What time is it?
It's not long after sunrise, maybe six.
Really? Wow.
It's a lot easier to wake up when you sleep on a pile of sticks and leaves.
You two stay warm last night?
Warm enough. Completely dry, though.

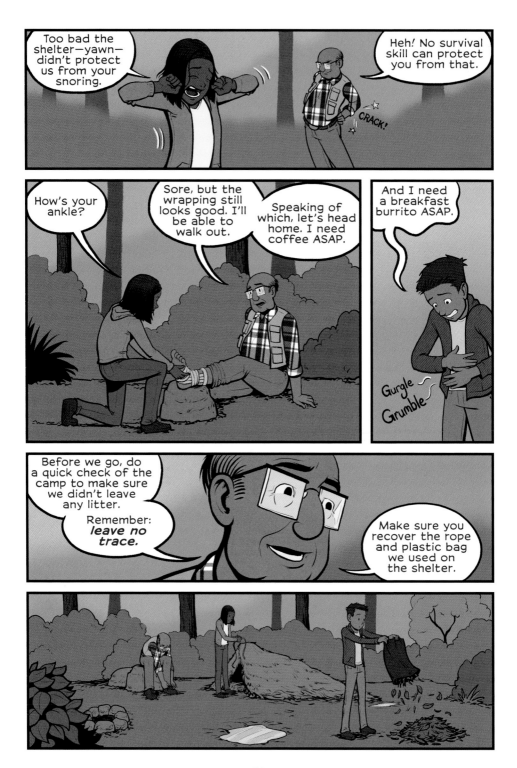

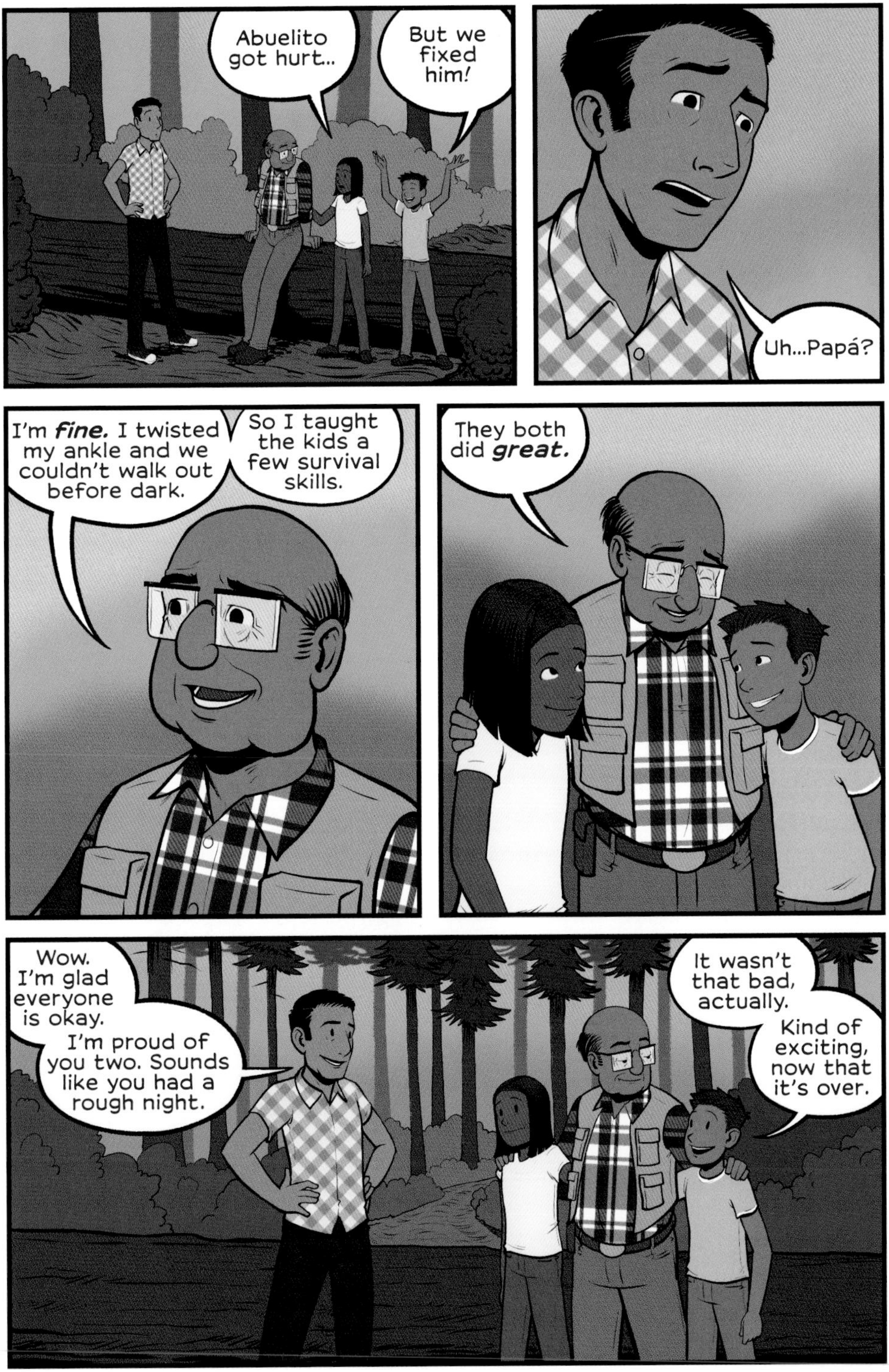
Abuelito got hurt...
But we fixed him!
Uh...Papá?
I'm *fine.* I twisted my ankle and we couldn't walk out before dark.
So I taught the kids a few survival skills.
They both did *great.*
Wow. I'm glad everyone is okay.
I'm proud of you two. Sounds like you had a rough night.
It wasn't that bad, actually.
Kind of exciting, now that it's over.

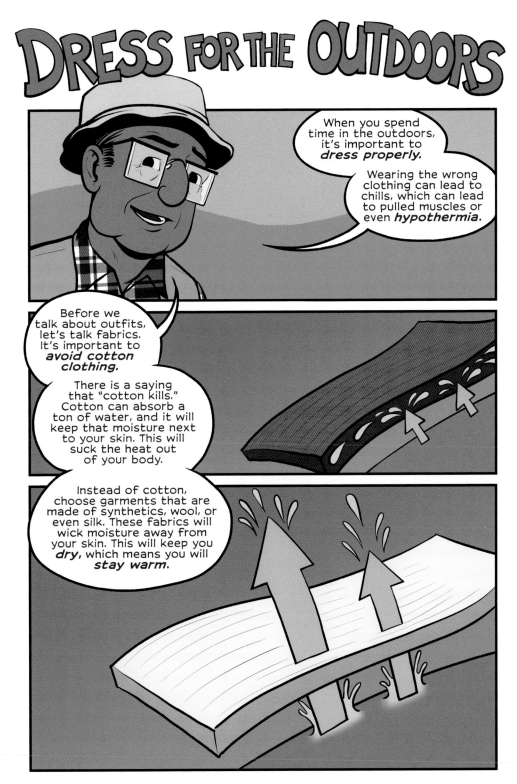

# DRESS FOR THE OUTDOORS

When you spend time in the outdoors, it's important to *dress properly.*

Wearing the wrong clothing can lead to chills, which can lead to pulled muscles or even *hypothermia.*

Before we talk about outfits, let's talk fabrics. It's important to *avoid cotton clothing.*

There is a saying that "cotton kills." Cotton can absorb a ton of water, and it will keep that moisture next to your skin. This will suck the heat out of your body.

Instead of cotton, choose garments that are made of synthetics, wool, or even silk. These fabrics will wick moisture away from your skin. This will keep you *dry,* which means you will *stay warm.*

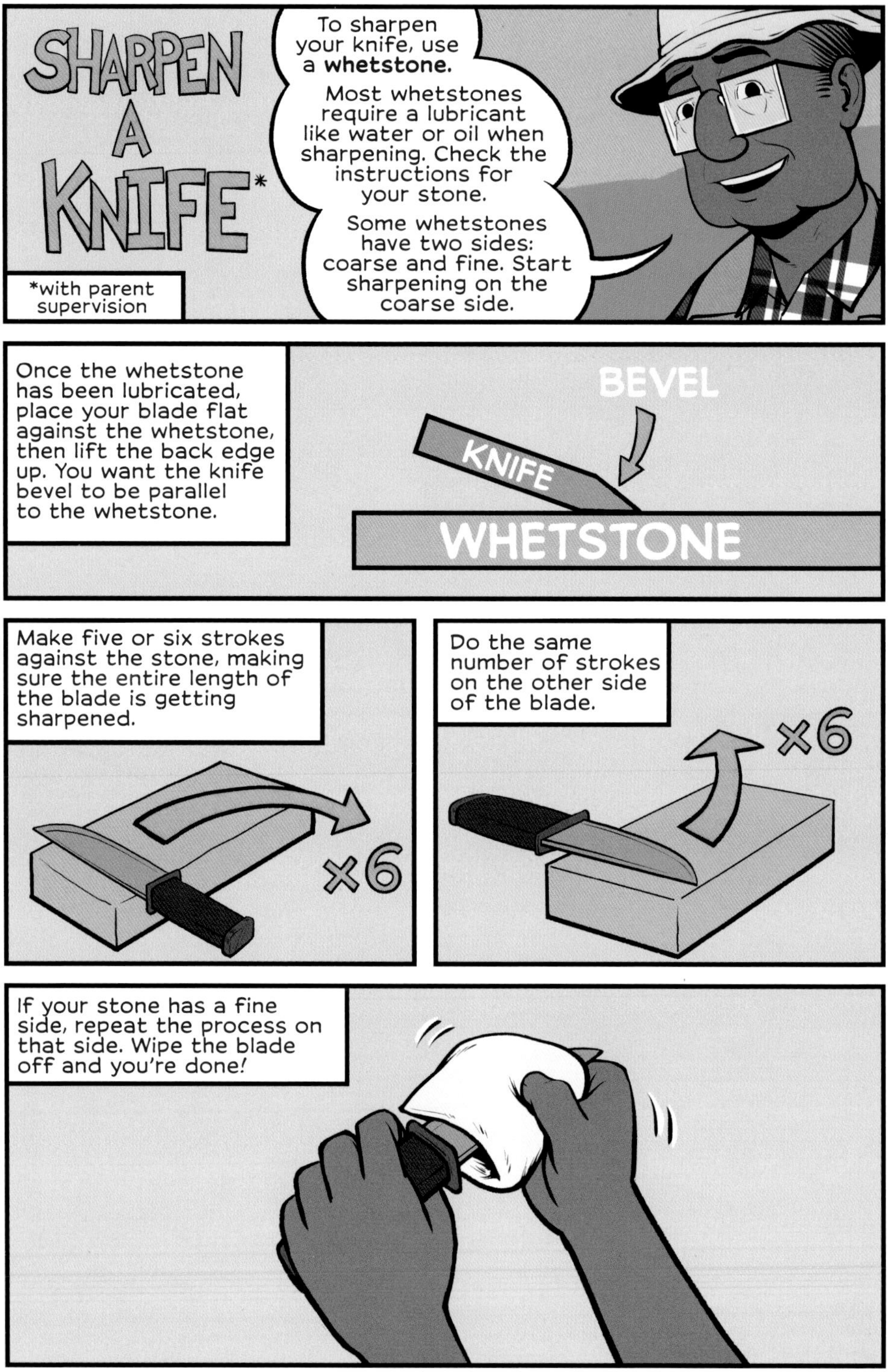
SHARPEN A KNIFE*
*with parent supervision
To sharpen your knife, use a **whetstone.**
Most whetstones require a lubricant like water or oil when sharpening. Check the instructions for your stone.
Some whetstones have two sides: coarse and fine. Start sharpening on the coarse side.
Once the whetstone has been lubricated, place your blade flat against the whetstone, then lift the back edge up. You want the knife bevel to be parallel to the whetstone.
BEVEL
KNIFE
WHETSTONE
Make five or six strokes against the stone, making sure the entire length of the blade is getting sharpened.
×6
Do the same number of strokes on the other side of the blade.
×6
If your stone has a fine side, repeat the process on that side. Wipe the blade off and you're done!

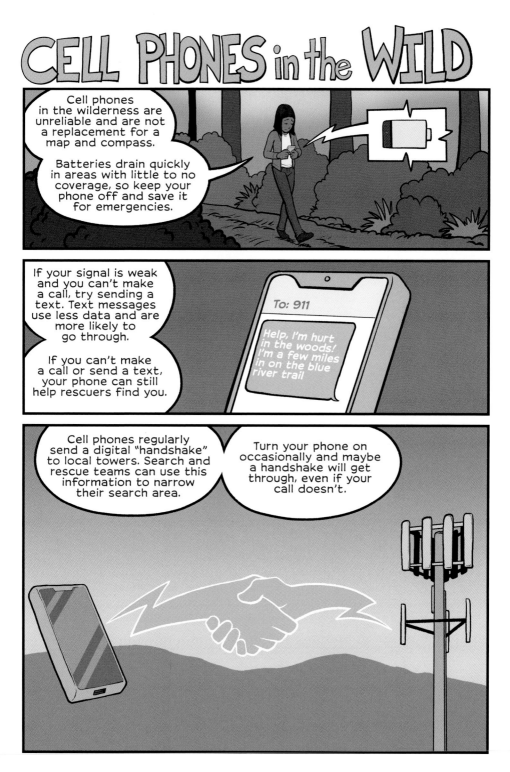

**First Second**

Published by First Second
First Second is an imprint of Roaring Brook Press,
a division of Holtzbrinck Publishing Holdings Limited Partnership
120 Broadway, New York, NY 10271
firstsecondbooks.com
mackids.com

Library of Congress Control Number: 2020919823

Our books may be purchased in bulk for promotional, educational, or business use.
Please contact your local bookseller or the Macmillan Corporate and Premium Sales Department at
(800) 221-7945 ext. 5442 or by email at MacmillanSpecialMarkets@macmillan.com.

First edition, 2021
Edited by Robyn Chapman, Bethany Bryan, and Alison Wilgus
Cover and interior book design by Molly Johanson
Expert consultation by Dan Wowak of Coalcracker Bushcraft
Printed in China by 1010 Printing International Limited, North Point, Hong Kong

ISBN 978-1-250-62066-8 (paperback)
1 3 5 7 9 10 8 6 4 2

ISBN 978-1-250-62065-1 (hardcover)
1 3 5 7 9 10 8 6 4 2

Drawn digitally in Clip Studio Paint and colored in Photoshop. Lettered with CCSoliloquous

Don't miss your next favorite book from First Second!
For the latest updates go to firstsecondnewsletter.com and sign up for our enewsletter.

Dedicated to my dad, uncles, and grandpa, for not laughing when I completely failed the lessons on page 102.

**Mike Lawrence** grew up camping, hunting, and fishing in the Sierra Nevada mountain range. In high school he moved to Oregon, where he went camping, hunting, and fishing in the Wallowa Mountains. He now lives in Portland, Oregon, and goes camping and fishing in the Cascade mountain range with his wife and two sons. Mike is the creator of the Star Scout series for First Second and was the illustrator of *Muddy Max: The Mystery of Marsh Creek*.